lbany Class A1a 2-8-4

Lima Locomotive Works in 1926

expressly for Mainline Modeler
by **Al Armitage**

Used by Permission

Scale: 3.5 mm = 1'

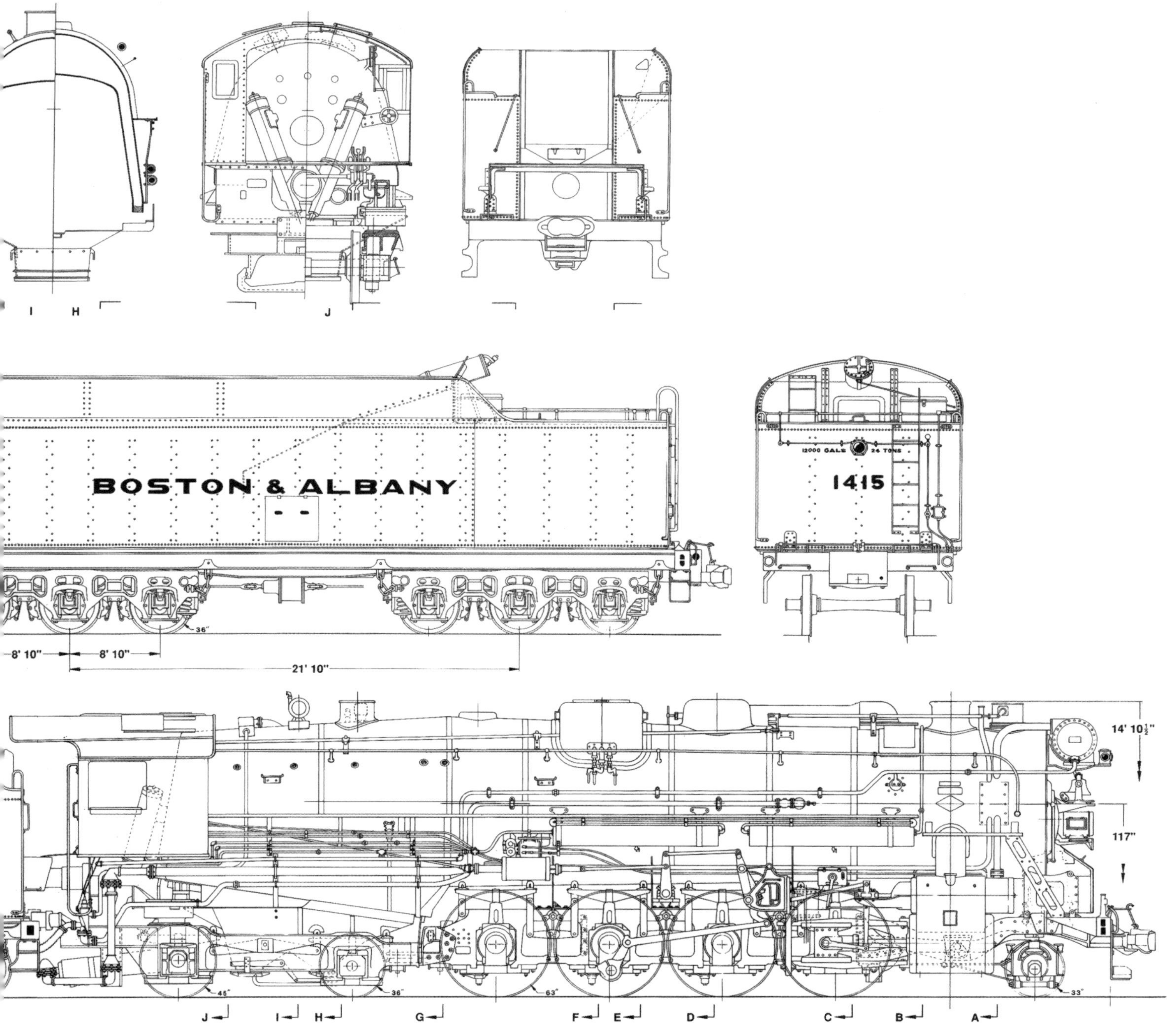

I H J

BOSTON & ALBANY

12000 GALS 24 TONS

1415

36"

8' 10" 8' 10"

21' 10"

14' 10½"

117"

45" 36" 63" 33"

J I H G F E D C B A

Lima Super Power Steam Locomotives

Thomas W. Dixon, Jr. and Kevin Kohls

with Karen Parker and Eugene L. Huddleston

Published 2010 by
TLC Publishing Inc.
18292 Forest Rd.
Forest, Virginia 24551
434-385-4076
www.tlcrailroadbooks.com

ISBN 9780939487967

Library of Congress Control Number 2010930023

Layout and Design by
Karen Parker

Printed in the U.S.A. by
Walsworth Printing Company, Marceline, Mo.

Cover: NKP 2-8-4 No. 757 with a manifest freight somewhere in the Midwest. (TLC Collection)

Previous Page: Lima built C&O class T-1 2-10-4 with Manifest train KD-92 at Milton, W.Va. in February, 1951. The first 2-10-4s to use drivers larger than 64", these powerful and fast locomotives were used on fast freight trains between Russell, Ky. and Hinton, W.Va. when the train length exceeded 75 cars. (Gene Huddleston photo, COHS Collection)

Back Cover:

C&O Class H-8 Allegheny (2-6-6-6) No. 1640 with a manifest eastbound at Alderson, W.Va. (photo by and courtesy of Charles Kerrigan);

Postcard image of a Southern Pacific Daylight 4-8-4 (courtesy of the Allen County Historical Society)

Reproduction of the Lima Builder's Plate of C&O 2-6-6-6 No. 1600 (photo by and used with permission of Scott Trostel)

Tourist Postcard of Lima, Ohio, touting the Lima Locomotive Works. (Courtesy of the Allen County Historical Society)

NKP 2-8-4 No. 753 on a turntable. (Jay Williams Collection)

Contents

Lima's First, Last, and Finest

Berkshire A-1, Lima's first Super Power locomotive, Nickel Plate 779, Lima's last Super Power locomotive, and C&O H-8 Allegheny, widely regarded as Lima's finest Super Power locomotive.

Introduction

The purpose of this book is to give an overview of the "modern" steam locomotives built by the Lima Locomotive Works of Lima, Ohio, beginning with its pioneering demonstrator A-1 2-8-4 in 1925 and ending with the Nickel Plate Road's 2-8-4 No. 779 of 1949. Photos are an important part of this work, as an additional purpose is to provide good builder photos as well as action views of these great machines as they looked both new and in actual service on the railroads that bought and used them during the last great era of the steam locomotive.

The evolution of the steam locomotive in America has been a matter of intense research and writing, especially so in the last 40 years, as historians, railroad enthusiasts, and modelers have focused on these grand, impressive, and historically important machines after the end of their last active service on major railroads in 1960.

More recently, attention has been drawn to the mechanical developments, design improvements, and operations of locomotives built from the 1920s through the 1940s, representing the most "modern" expression of boiler and firebox design, appliances, and ancillary devices, which brought the reciprocating steam locomotive to its peak in efficiency, and some say in looks. This was the era of "big steam," but more broadly "big, powerful, and fast" steam, which would challenge the emerging technology of the diesel-electric locomotive for a few years, and then fall before its obvious advantages.

"Super Power," or "Superpower" is an appellation generally given to steam locomotives built after 1925 that have a firebox significantly larger than generally used prior to that time, usually located entirely behind the driving wheels and supported by a four-wheel (and in one case a 6-wheel) trailing truck. This larger firebox allowed significantly more coal to be burned more efficiently, as compared to a firebox that was located between the drivers or above them. Along with other improvements, this allowed for the creation of furnaces and boilers that could supply a large volume of steam that could not be exhausted by use in the cylinders during sustained operation at high speed. The word "Super Power" was coined by Lima as part of its advertising campaign for this new concept. However, the word can be applied to locomotives of this general concept and design constructed by any of the commercial builders of the era, the other two principal companies being Baldwin Locomotive Works, and the American Locomotive Company (Alco) (as well as at least two types built by Norfolk & Western Railway in its own shops).

In fact, both Alco and Baldwin built more locomotives to the Super Power design than did Lima itself, because much of the design was not proprietary, but was simply a concept of how to put together and to size existing standard locomotive parts and practices.

Lima itself began by building the small geared Shay type engines that were used in logging and some industrial applications, but by 1904 the company began to build rod locomotives, first small engines for the same type of buyers as those purchasing its Shays. Then by the WWI-era it was building larger power for major railroads, and by the 1920s was challenging the other two large builders for a share of the overall market for large locomotives being marketed to Class I railroads. Lima was always third in size of the three big steam builders.

Number of Superpower Locomotives built by the Major Commercial Builders

Engine Type	Baldwin	Alco	Lima	RR Shops	Total	RRs Using
4-4-4	0	0	0	1	1	1
4-6-4	75	289	14	27	405	15
2-8-4	75	166	368	0	609	17
4-8-4	383	330	96	108	917	31
2-10-4	106	20	141	125	392	9
2-6-6-4	17	0	0	43	60	3
4-6-6-4	27	225	0	0	252	9
2-8-8-4	254	1	12	0	267	4
4-8-8-4	0	25	0	0	25	1
2-6-6-6	0	0	68	0	68	2
Totals	937	1,056	699	304	2,996	

This book will only cover Super Power locomotives built by Lima. The products of the other companies that fit the Super Power mold will not be covered. Although the locomotives built by Baldwin and Alco were certainly as well appreciated in their time as those built by Lima, when the name Super Power is mentioned, Lima is most often brought to mind, not only because it originated the concept but because it popularized the name, and its last decades of work were devoted to bringing the concept to its highest and final expression and conclusion. This conclusion was really also the culmination of the era of the reciprocating steam locomotive.

In this book we will generally use the word "locomotive" to mean the entire machine, including the boiler, cab, cylinders, driving and other wheels, and tender. The word "engine" is usually applied to the main machinery minus the tender, but it can also mean just a set of cylinders connected to driving wheels when speaking of an articulated locomotive.

This work was conceived by Kevin Kohls based his collection of Lima builder photos, and by Tom Dixon, because of his interest in the modern steam locomotive. It owes much to Gene Huddleston, whose understanding of the Super Power design, especially as it was practiced in the locomotives built by Lima for the Chesapeake & Ohio Railway, was key in explaining the concept. Karen Parker, whose recent book *How a Steam Locomotive Works*, not only did the layout and design for the book, but also made a marked contribution in the text and captions based on her wide knowledge and understanding of the physics, mechanics, and history of the steam locomotive in America.

We wish to thank those who helped with photos, particular Jay Williams and Harold Vollrath, and to those living and dead, whose photography graces these pages. The Allen County Historical Society of Lima also supplied valuable assistance and photos.

The book is divided into sections, based on the Lima construction for individual railroads. The first part of the book includes the original A-1 and its direct descendents, locomotives whose design closely followed that of Lima's Super Power pioneer. Most of the second half the book is devoted to four lines, the Chesapeake & Ohio, Nickel Plate (NYC&St.L), Pere Marquette, and Erie because they purchased most of their Super Power steam under the control and guidance of a central authority. The four lines were controlled by the Van Sweringen financiers of Cleveland, and though operated as separate companies, their mechanical work was controlled by a unified committee called the Advisory Mechanical Committee (AMC). The explanation of this committee and it work is followed by sections on the four railroads. The Virginian Railway's 2-6-6-6s and 2-8-4s are also treated in this section since they are almost exact copies of Van Sweringen AMC designs. Also in this section are the remaining later Super Power designs.

Thomas W. Dixon, Jr.

Kevin Kohls

Eugene L. Huddleston

Karen Parker

One may very well ask what were the prime considerations in building steam locomotives before the Lima Super Power concept came to the fore in 1925.

An event that had a lasting effect on the development of American steam locomotives was the U. S. entry into World War I. Soon after entry into the war it became obvious that the railroads could not meet the needs for getting men and materiel to the ports of embarkation, so the federal government seized the railroads and put them under the control of the United States Railroad Administration (USRA).

In addition to assuming operational control of the various lines to eliminate congestion through coordinated action, the USRA set up a committee to design new standardized cars and locomotives. As a result, it produced a series of designs that were created by the best mechanical engineering minds of the era both from the major builders and from several railroads. These twelve designs in eight different wheel arrangements, though promulgated after the end of hostilities in the war, were built and allocated to numerous railroads because the USRA continued to control the nation's railroads until 1920. So well respected were these designs that they were copied and used frequently in the decade following. Other designs were based on the USRA locomotives, but further refined or modified to fit the particular needs of the roads ordering them. Over 1,800 "USRA" type locomotives were built.

Although the USRA locomotives represented the best concepts then available and offered the virtue of standardization both in construction and in replacement parts, the railroads soon returned to their own design concepts, and the decade of the 1920s became one of innovation and trial, part of which led to Super Power.

An important innovation of the early 1920s was the completely butt-welded firebox, which allowed for better and larger internal combustion chambers, which in turn allowed for better combustion of gases before they entered the tubes and flues.

The Mikado type reached its maximum development during the early 1920s as well. Both the Delaware, Lackawanna & Western and the Chesapeake & Ohio purchased 2-8-2s that had or exceeded 67,000 pounds in tractive effort, with 63-inch drivers.

Also during the 1920s, some notable three-cylinder types were tried, with some successes, including a number of stout engines built for the Southern Pacific and Union Pacific, but because of maintenance issues involving the third cylinder, which was hung under the smokebox and connected to the driving axles by a cranked axle, they never gained wide acceptance.

An important technological advancement of about 1923 was the introduction of a one-piece engine bed frame, which soon largely replaced the built-up frames that were susceptible to constant maintenance. Eventually the cylinders themselves were also cast as integral parts of this one-piece cast frame. Of course, on articulated locomotives, the cast frame was actually in two pieces, linked together by a swivel. Other experiments in the era included water-tube fireboxes and boilers and high-pressure boilers.

The Superheater was developed in about 1905, and it become a standard application by the 1920s, as well as the mechanical stoker, improved feedwater heaters and injectors, and, the booster which was applied not only to the trailing engine truck but sometimes to trucks under the tender. The Superheater was a device consisting of a series of tubes through which steam was passed and further heated to a higher temperature before being delivered to the cylinders.

Outside forces were beginning to have an effect on railroading in the 1920s as well. The most important of these was the rise of the automobile, bus, and motor-truck, and ever-improving highways over which they could travel. The effect on railroads was enough to convince them that they needed to pay more attention to speed as well as reliable on-time performance, and convenient scheduling to retain passenger business. With regard to freight the need for speedy, reliable transportation became steadily more important, so that the concern with carrying heavier and heavier trains receded in importance. Speed and reliability again became important to compete with truckers, who were beginning to become strong competitors, at least in shorter-distance markets.

With all this as background the stage was set for some new idea that would further help the railroads in what would become a very much changed competitive environment going through the 1930s and leading up to World War II. Of course this period was interrupted by the dislocations caused by the Great Depression, the effects of which really were only ameliorated by the coming of war.

Lima, the "Other" Locomotive Builder

By the turn of the 20th Century the several locomotive building companies in the United States were essentially consolidated into two builders, Baldwin Locomotive Works of Eddystone (Philadelphia), and American Locomotive Company, which was a consolidation of several builders at various locations, but with its principal headquarters and largest facility at Schenectady, New York. However, there was a third builder, which had made its reputation building the Shay geared locomotive, used mainly in logging operations: the Lima Locomotive Works of Lima, Ohio (pronounced L-eye-ma, rather than Lee-ma as in Peru.)

The Lima Machine Works, in the 1870's was building sawmill equipment, and in the late 1870s it started producing the new geared locomotive designed by Ephraim Shay of Michigan to handle transportation of logs from the woods to his saw mill. The concept of the locomotive was a standard boiler connected with cylinders, but instead of the cylinders being placed horizontally and driving large wheels through means of long rods, they were placed vertically, on one side of the boiler. The pistons drove a rod that connected with a crank on a drive shaft that ran the entire length of the locomotive on one side, This was equipped with gears that meshed with gears on the side of the wheels carrying the locomotive in sets of 4-wheel trucks. These wheels were small in diameter, usually no more than 36 inches. This design, though unconventional looking, supplied a huge amount of power for the train, and was very flexible to traverse the roughly laid logging railroads that usually had no ballast, were laid with light rail (even sometimes laid with wooden logs instead of iron or steel rails), on un-graded, un-prepared routes with steep grades and maximum curvature. The Shay also had a very short rigid wheel-base: just the distance between the axles on one of the trucks. The entire weight of the Shay also was on its driving wheels because the drive shaft extended to all wheels under the locomotive. Most Shays carried no tender, but had a coal and water bunker positioned behind the cab as part of the engine structure. Later water tenders were added to larger examples,

Aerial view showing the huge plant of the Lima Locomotive Works at Lima, Ohio, in its heyday. B&O ran north-south beside the plant, Erie crossed the NKP and B&O, all within sight of the large plant. (Lima Photo, Kevin Kohls Collection)

which were also fitted with geared power trucks that were likewise connected to the main driving crankshaft.

The design, though not alone among geared locomotive types, enjoyed large success after the turn of the 20th Century and became the most commonly used geared locomotive type. Competitors included the Climax and Heisler designs.

By the late 1880s Lima also was building occasional conventional rod locomotives, mostly for short lines. In 1903, a huge Shay was built for the Chesapeake & Ohio, one of the few Class I railroads to operate Shays. It found these locomotives suitable for several of its coal-producing branch lines in the mountainn of West Virginia. This would acquaint C&O with Lima, and in the 1930s-1940s C&O became one of Lima's principal customers for its Super Power locomotives.

However, though Lima's main product continued to be Shays, it also produced a number of small rod locomotives in the form of light industrial switchers. However, it shipped its first locomotives to Class I railroads in 1911-12 with 0-6-0s for the Southern Railway, and 0-8-0s for Delaware, Lackawanna & Western, as well as 4-6-2s for the Erie in 1912. In the following years larger rod locomotives were built for Lackawanna, New York Central, Erie, Great Northern, Illinois Central, Central of Georgia and others, and also an articulated Mallet for the Western Maryland (a 2-8-8-2) in 1915. During the USRA-era Lima built numerous USRA-designed locomotives. All of Lima's engines had a reputation as good quality machines that put in excellent performances.

It was good thing that Lima began building large rod locomotives, as the market for Shays soon dried up. There was a lively second-hand market in these locomotives, as one lumber operation was depleted and went out of business, its locomotives were often sold to another. In addition, there were fewer and fewer new large logging operations opening up as the major virgin forests that were easily accessible were logged-out. Shays continued to be built, but on a very limited scale compared with earlier quantities.

William E. Woodard was born in Utica, New York in 1873, and received his degree in mechanical engineering from Cornell University in 1896. He worked at Baldwin Locomotive Company, Cramp Shipyard, Dickson Locomotive Works, Schenectady Locomotive Works, and American Locomotive Company (into which company Dickson and Schenectady were merged). Finally he came to Lima in 1916 with its change in management and new outlook. When he moved to the Lima position as Vice-President and a director of the company, he continued to live in New York, operating from Lima's office at 60 E. 42nd Street in New York City.

Known as "Will," he soon became the driving force behind Lima's innovative approach to the "new" era of locomotive design, and his name would forever be linked with the Super Power concept and implementation.

Woodard was the leader of Lima's "brain trust"; others who worked with him and contributed to the development of the early Super Power locomotives included Herb Snyder, who worked at Lima rather than in New York as Woodard did, and George Basford, a consultant who worked with Woodard in New York. W.H. Winterrowd also was part of this team, initially working at Lima as the "Assistant Secretary", but later taking the position of VP of Engineering when Woodard took the title of VP of Design.

In 1916 Joel S. Coffin, owner of the Superheater Company and Franklin Railway Supply Company, both of which produced appliances for use in building steam locomotives, acquired control of Lima from its previous owners, and brought with him a group of experienced executives and engineers, most of whom came from various plants operated by Alco. Included in this group of men was a mechanical engineer named William E. Woodard, who came from Alco's main plant at Schenectady. It was Woodard who would become the "father" of Super Power.

In 1923 Lima's new management completed a new, modern plant that would give it room for an expanded place among the nation's locomotive builders.

Super Power's Precursor – The NYC H-10

It was in 1922 that Lima's 2-8-2, built as a company owned experimental demonstrator, but lettered as New York Central's Class H-10 and numbered 8000, would begin a revolution in locomotive design thinking. Up to this time the thinking of railroads was to opt for tractive power to haul maximum loads at relatively slow speeds, and for the designers at the major builders to concentrate on increasing power in the form of tractive effort. They could do this by tinkering with the cylinder diameter or driver size, but they had largely neglected the need for a boiler that could supply a good, constant, and consistent supply of steam to those cylinders in all conditions for which it was intended to be used. In other words a "free steaming" boiler that would not run out of steam no matter how much was used in its cylinders. Some designs of the era actually did experience problems of running out of steam even at medium speeds.

New York Central was one of the railroads that was building new locomotives to meet demands of the booming traffic of the 1920s and also to replace older power that had been designed for the earlier era of railroading. NYC was involved in extensive testing as well, and was an ideal road to work with Lima to develop new designs.

It is now generally recognized by historians that Lima's close coordination with NYC designers resulted in the creation of the pre-Super Power prototype in the form of NYC's Class H-10 2-8-2, built at Lima in 1921-22. By this time William E. Woodard, was behind Lima's design work.

Woodard realized that locomotives had about reached their maximum size given weight and clearance limitations on most railroads, so the only way to improve power and efficiency was to design within existing limitations. To accomplish this he believed that applying and improving certain appliances and auxiliary devices would help improve the performance of locomotives with existing size limitations. He also saw that the generation of a sufficient supply of steam through the construction of a boiler/firebox of appropriate proportions and output was key to creation of a locomotive that could deliver a high power (tractive power and horsepower), for sustained

LIMA LOCOMOTIVE WORKS NO. 8000 ORDER NO. 1027

DELIVERED	8000: JUNE, 1922	CONSTRUCTION NUMBER	6242

WHEEL ARRANGEMENT	DRIVING WHEEL DIAMETER	CYLINDERS		BOILER		FIREBOX		
		DIAMETER	STROKE	DIAMETER	PRESSURE	LENGTH	WIDTH	GRATE AREA
2-8-2	63"	28"	30"	86"	200 p.s.i.	114 ⅛"	84¼"	66.4 SQ.FT.

WHEEL BASE			TRACTIVE POWER	FACTOR OF ADHESION		TUBES AND FLUES		
DRIVING	ENGINE	ENGINE AND TENDER	MAIN CYLINDERS WITH BOOSTER			NUMBER	DIAMETER	LENGTH
16' 6"	37' 0"	71' 6½"	63,500 lbs. 74,500 lbs.	3.87		253	3¼"	20' 0"

AVERAGE WEIGHT IN WORKING ORDER, POUNDS				HEATING SURFACES, SQUARE FEET				
ON DRIVERS	TRUCK	TRAILER	TOTAL ENGINE	FLUES	FIREBOX	ARCH TUBES	TOTAL	SUPERHEATER
245,500	30,000	58,500	334,000	4,287	223	68	4,578	1,780

TENDER			
TYPE	FUEL	WATER	WEIGHT, FULLY LOADED
8 WHEEL	16 TONS	10,000 GALS	199,700 LBS.

periods and at relatively higher speeds than before attained on most railroads in freight operations. Other locomotive designers usually looked on the auxiliary devices such as super heaters and feedwater heaters, as not really a part of the locomotive's overall design.

With the NYC 2-8-2 Woodard proved otherwise, especially with regard to the superheater. By improving its design to add half again more superheating surface he was able to give the H-10 hotter and dryer steam which in turn allowed more power to be generated with this steam at the cylinders. Likewise the feedwater heater was added and improved so as to get more efficiency out of the boiler. A combustion chamber, then coming into use, was not applied because of size limitations, but the locomotive was equipped with an improved double brick arch supported by eight 3-½-inch tubes. This assisted in the fuller combustion of gases much in the way that a combustion chamber would. Some designers of the era felt that the combustion chamber would not improve a locomotive's performance because it caused shortening of flues and tubes. Only later was the design developed to the point that it could be shown that the combustion chamber added significantly more efficiency to the boiler. Over time as locomotives continued to increase in size, especially the articulated designs, enough room was available to include a combustion chamber at the same time provide for tubes that were at the maximum considered appropriate at about 20-25 feet.

Lima also applied the front-end throttle attached to the Superheater header and provided a dry pipe that carried steam from the steam dome to the superheater on the outside top of the boiler. The dome was also moved to the second boiler course, placing it closer to the front end of the locomotive and reducing the distance that steam had to travel upon leaving the dome. The dome and the pipe were cast integrally.

A Franklin C-1 booster was added to the trailing truck so as to add power for starting heavy

Lima builder's photos of the right side of the No. 8000 and left side of the virtually identical NYC H-10a No. 1. Lima built the 8000 with thier own funds in June, 1922, and it operated in test service on the Michigan Central as a company owned experimental demonstrator, although lettered for the New York Central. So successful were those tests that the New York Central bought the locomotive from Lima in August, 1922 and ordered 150 virtual duplicates as well. (Allen County Historical Society Collection)

trains. This generated 11,000 pounds of tractive effort up to 15 mph.

The various changes that Lima incorporated into the new 2-8-2 increased its weight over the older NYC 2-8-2s by only about three tons. This caused some problems because it altered the factor of adhesion and made the locomotive slippery. The actual factor of adhesion was 3.87 vs. the "ideal" of design target of 4.0

In actual testing on NYC after delivery of the new locomotive, it showed a marked improvement in performance over the line's older Mikados. Importantly it showed a 77% boiler efficiency (amount of water converted to steam for fuel burned), which was better than any existing locomotive of the time. Also, indicated drawbar horsepower was more than 25% better than the earlier 2-8-2s. These performance results were achieved while operating at train speeds more than double what was usually achieved. It was given No. 8000 and sub-lettered for NYC subsidiary Michigan Central.

Railway Age, in its August 5, 1922 issue says the following about the new locomotive:

> "When a railroad buys a locomotive differing radically from those in service and after testing it for scarcely more than a month, buys 150 more identically like it, no further proof is needed that new design has made good. The order placed by New York Central last week is one of the noteworthy events of recent years and one that is likely to have a decided effect on motive power policies and on operating practice. . . . The leading features of the design are maximum power per unit of weight, minimum fuel consumption and ease of operation. . . . These improvements are often discussed by engineers but up to this time have been too seldom applied as effectively as they might be to reduce the cost of operation. When as in this type, the higher officers co-operate in designing a type that will meet the operating requirements and then give the motive power a chance to perform at its best efficiency, the savings that can be effected are remarkable. The New York Central's latest type of power is likely to be the forerunner of many designs of improved locomotives."

A locomotive's "factor of adhesion" is simply the ratio of the rated tractive effort to the weight on drivers. If this value is too low, the locomotive will, at times, spin its drivers because it is exerting too much force on the rail, breaking the friction between the tires and the railhead. If it is too high, this is an indication that the engine has more pulling potential than it is rated for. This value was usually reported using two digits to the right of the decimal point, and the ideal value was 4.00, indicating that the drawbar pull is ¼ of the weight on the drivers. Values in the range from 3.80 to 4.20 were commonly found, and occasionally as low as 3.5 (a very slippery engine) and as high as 4.5 (an engine that usually could reliably pull more than it was rated for).

Indeed it was! The *Railway Age* editor had rightly summed up the issue and saw that this was the future for locomotive design. Woodard, Lima, and NYC had collaborated on something new and they were successful. But Woodard was not about to rest with this success, he still had many ideas in mind for further development along the lines that had been started.

It was this huge success with the new concepts and its wholehearted acceptance by powerful and conservative New York Central that literally awakened the whole locomotive industry to the fact that a new era of locomotive design was at hand.

Dawn of Super Power - The A-1

The next logical step in the mind of Woodard and Lima designers was the use of a 4-wheel trailing truck to support an enlarged firebox, providing for a significantly larger grate area, and thus assisting in creating the "free steaming" locomotive that would be the key to Super Power.

Woodard outlined much of the Super Power concept in an article in *Railway Age* for January 24, 1925:

> "Railway operating officers have for some time realized the importance of increased horsepower output from their locomotives as a factor in improving their operating conditions. This is known to them under different names. The operating man may see it as ton-mile-hours; it may become evident to him in increased speed of trains or increate in the number of cars per train, but every such increase means to him a decreased operating radio and greater capacity for his line. . . .
>
> . . . The use of higher pressure is one way in which this demand is being met. . . . The use of limited cut-off in the cylinders to produce high horsepower. . . . It is idle to design a fine engine and driving mechanism with-

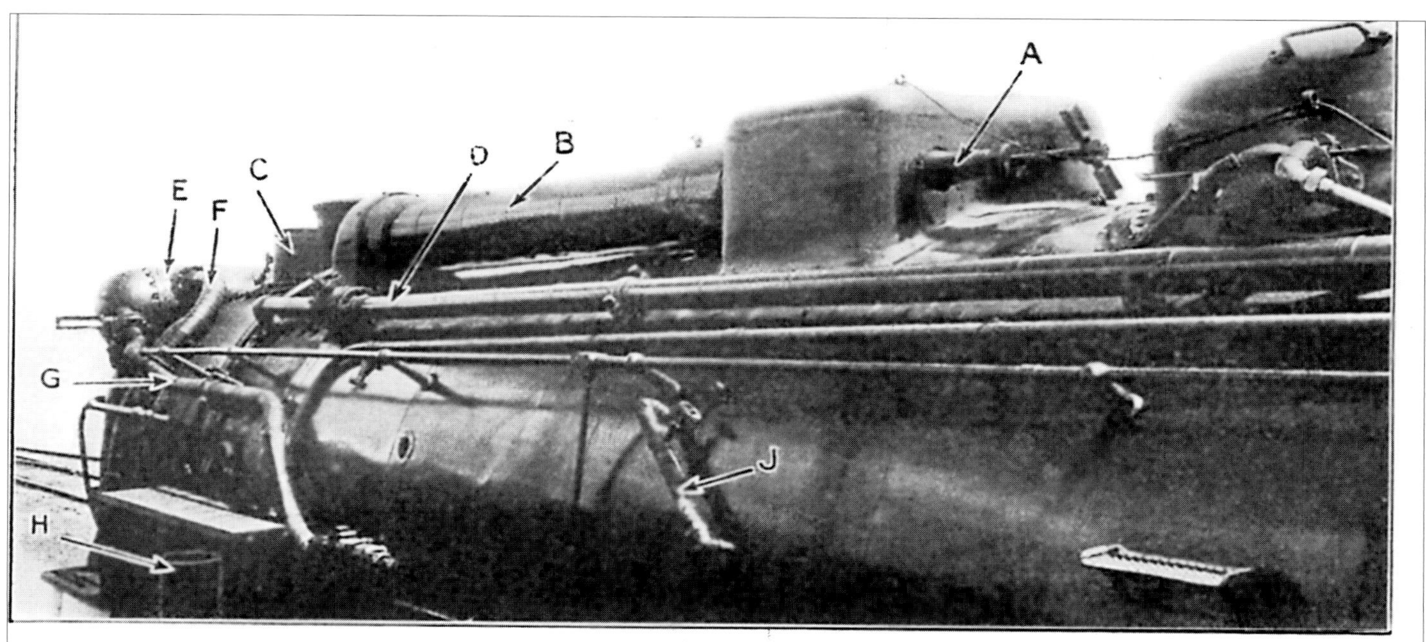

Forward End of Boiler from Left Side

A, Shut-off Valve; *B*, Outside Steam Pipe; *C*, Throttle; *D*, Superheated Steam Pipe to Turret; *E*, Feedwater Heater; *F*, Exhaust Steam Pipe to Heater; *G*, Feedwater Discharge Pipe from Heater; *H*, Feedwater Pump; *J*, Drain Pipe from Steam Separator.

This photo of the left side top of No. 8000's boiler clearly shows the outside dry pipe, the pipe for taking superheated steam back to the turret in front of the cab, the front end throttle, and the feedwater heater, all novel features in 1922 when the locomotive was built. (Railway Age, *Vol. 73, No. 10, September 2, 1922)*

This drawing of No. 8000 has the firebox shaded, clearly indicating that Woodard did not include a combustion chamber at the front of the firebox in the design, although the USRA light and heavy Mikados designed just two years earlier included one, as did vriturally every Super Power locomotive built after 1930. (Railway Review, *September 12, 1925)*

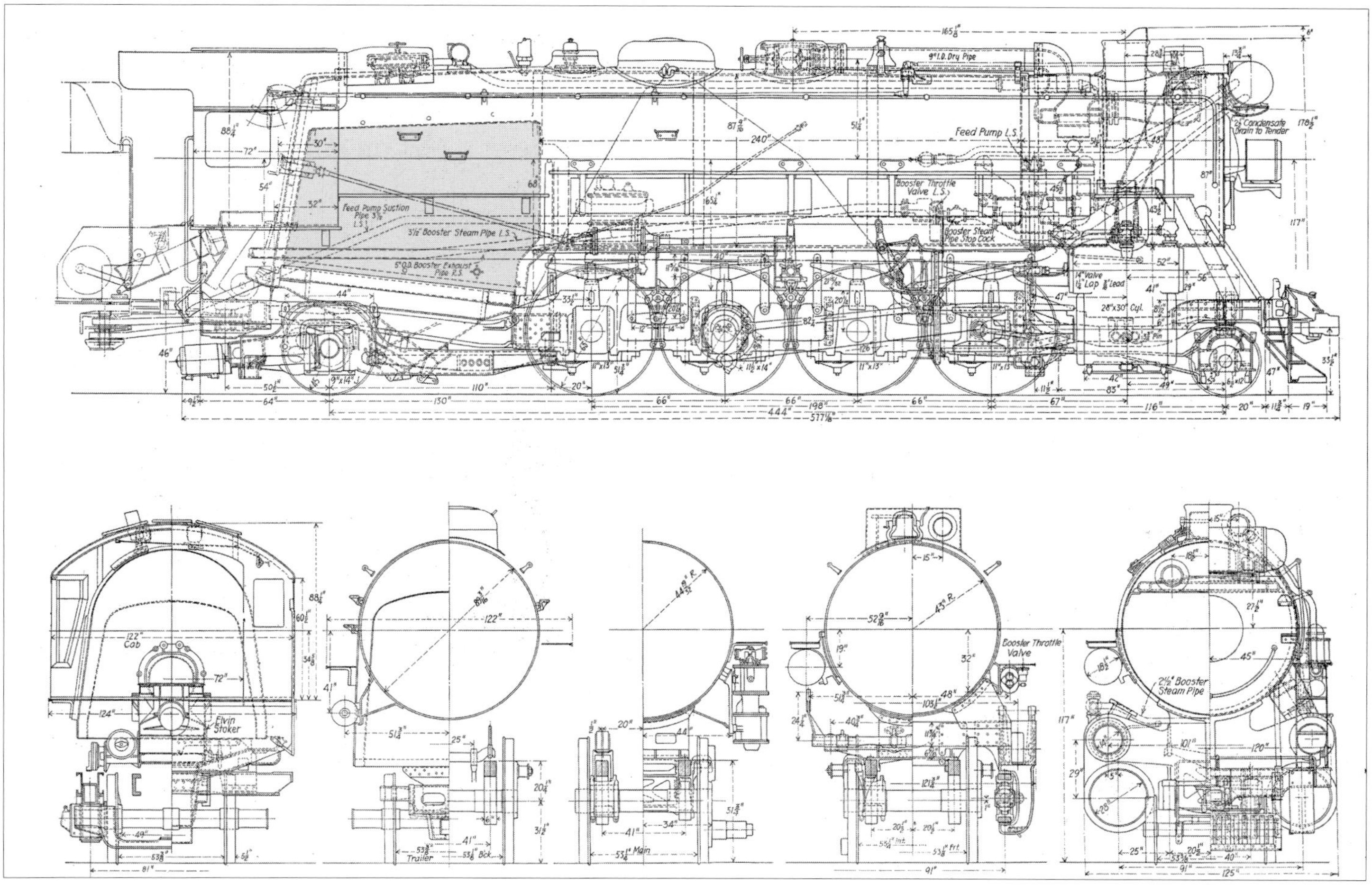

out proper means to feed it. . . . We have again come to the . . . Point in the evolution of the locomotive; we have reached the limit of the grate which we can carry on a two-wheeled training truck. . . . So we are ready for the next step, which is the four-wheel trailer and the big firebox.

My vision of the locomotive of the near future is one with a high boiler pressure, cylinders capable of developing 3,000 to 3,500 hp., with a boiler and firebox which are capable of producing an adequate amount of steam for the cylinders in an economical manner. Such locomotives will have larger fireboxes than we are accustomed to use. The coal will be burned at a low rate of combustion giving a high boiler efficiency. They will have a large gas area through the flues and tubes to match the firebox. They will produce these high horsepowers at relatively low rates of steam consumption. Such engines are not a dream; they will be here soon."

As early as March 1923 Lima officials give public acknowledgment to the fact that they were working on a design with a four-wheel trailer. For the next two years Lima engineers worked on the refinement of things contained in the NYC H-10 and the end result was a new 2-8-4. This was the first 2-8-4 wheel arrangement locomotive ever built.

The number "A-1" was given since the locomotive was built on the company's account as a demonstrator/experimental and not for any particular railroad, though it would eventually be sold to the Illinois Central which bought 50 2-8-4s of almost identical design.

Alfred Bruce in his book *The Steam locomotive in America* (1952) says of the A-1: "This experimental 2-8-4-type engine with 63-in. drivers was designed to produce high-horsepower output at medium speeds. It was an outstanding locomotive in many respects and influenced nearly all subsequent design work on large engines."

NYC continued to cooperate with Woodard and Lima by testing several of the features that were proposed for the new locomotive, as they had done with their own H-10 before, but they did not commit to buy the new design, so it was built as a "stock" locomotive on Lima's own account. In the meantime NYC ordered a total of 300 of the new style 2-8-2s for several of its component lines, from various builders, using Lima's design as the standard.

Lima completed this new experimental locomotive and sent it to test on the Boston & Albany in February 1925. *Railway Age* in its May 2, 1925 issue fully covered the new locomotive. Some of what was said in that article is repro-

Right and Left side builder's photos of the A-1, lettered for the Boston & Albany, where it had its initial testing. (Allen County Historical Society Collection)

duced herewith:

" The principal objectives in the design of this locomotive were the development of high horsepower capacity and improved economy in the use of fuel. It may be considered the logical step forward in carrying out the principals on which this builder has been working since the inception of the design of Locomotive 8000, which was built for the Michigan Central in 1922, and of which design over 300 have been built for various parts of the New York Central System. A comparison of the more important dimensions and proportions of the two locomotives will serve to indicate the methods by which it is expected to obtain increased horsepower and higher fuel economy. Such a comparison will be found in the table.

	A-1	8000	USRA Heavy 2-8-2
Type	2-8-4	2-8-2	2-8-2
Cylinders, diameter & stroke	28 by 30	28 by 30	27x32
Cut-off in full gear	60 per cent	Full stroke	Full stroke
Boiler pressure	240 lb.	200 lb.	190 psi
Weights, in working order			
On drivers	248,200 lb.	245,500 lb.	240,000 lb.
On front truck	35,500 lb.	30,000 lb.	28,000 lbs.
On Trailing Truck	101,300 lb.	58,500 lb.	57,000 lbs
Total engine	385,000 lb.	334,000 lb.	325,000 lbs
Diameter of drivers	63 in.	63 in.	63 in
Heating surfaces:			
Firebox, incl. Arch tubes	337 sq. ft.	291 sq. ft.	319 sq.ft.
Tubes and flues	4,773 sq. ft.	4,287 sq. ft.	3,978 sq.ft.
Total evaporative	5,110 sq. ft.	4,578 sq. ft.	4,297 sq.ft.
Superheating	2,111 sq. ft.	1,780 sq. ft.	993 sq.ft.
Combined evaporative and Superheating	7,221 sq. ft.	6,358 sq. ft.	5,290 sq.ft.
Grate area	100 sq. ft.	66.4 sq. ft.	70.8 sq.ft.
Net gas area through tubes and flues	10.66 sq. ft.	9.3 sq. ft.	11.84 sq.ft.
Rated tractive force:			
Engine	69,400 lb.	63,500 lb.	60,000 lb.
Engine and booster	82,600 lb.	74,500 lb.	60,000 lb.
Factor of adhesion	3.58	3.87	4.0

It will be seen that the cylinders are the same size on both locomotives. This suggests that an increase in tractive force was not the primary objective, although some increase has been possible because of the smoother torque curve and the resulting lower factor of adhesion which the employment of limited cut-off made possible. The outstanding difference in proportions is in the size of the grates, the new 2-8-4 locomotive having approximately 50 per cent more grate area than did the earlier Mikado. It will also be noted that the boiler is somewhat larger in other respects. The total evaporative heating surface has been increased in the amount of superheating surface, resulting in an increase of combined evaporative and superheating surface of about 13½ per cent. While these figures indicate a considerable increase in capacity for heat absorption, the greatest increase in boiler capacity will undoubtedly result from the ability to release at the grate a large aggregate amount of heat at exceptionally low rates of combustion. This favors both high boiler capacity and high fuel economy.

The other principal factor in this design for the improvement of fuel economy is the employment of the limited maximum cut-off which is accompanied by an increase in boiler pressure to offset the reduction in the ratio of mean effective pressure to initial pressure resulting from the limited cut-off. While the value of the limited cut-off as an economy factor is more apparent within the speed range at which full-stroke cut-off locomotives are ordinarily operated, it has also been found that a significant reduction in water rate occurs throughout the entire speed range. For freight service, a very considerable percentage of the locomotive mileage is made in the speed range within which full-stroke locomotives operate at more than 60 per cent cut-off.

. . . [Its] construction embodies four important innovations in detail design. . . . These are the cast steel cylinders, which have made possible a saving of 4,000 lb. In weight; the articulated four-wheel trailing truck which does not require rear frame extensions and has made possible a marked improvement in ash pan design; the articulated main rod which delivers its load on two crank pins instead of on one, and the simple port arrangement by which an unbalanced cut-off has been obtained in the two ends of the cylinders at starting, with a resulting increase in the smoothness of the starting torque curve.

. . . The articulated four-wheel trailing truck is a unique development in the design of frame and the equalizer systems. The truck in effect forms a part of the main frame system, leaving no need for rear frame extensions back of the main frame. The main frames terminate just rear of the rear pair of drivers. Between them is bolted a hinge casting of the Mallet type; a corresponding hinge casting forms the front member of the trailer truck. . . . . The vertical load is transmitted to the trailer truck at two points on each side. . . . While the trailer truck is free to swing laterally about its hinge joint, its vertical alignment remains unchanged with respect to the main frames which, in effect, it forms a part.

. . . The ash pan, instead of being applied directly to the mud ring, is built into the trailer truck and when the trailer truck is removed from the locomotive the ash pan is removed with it. The width of the flare required to keep the ash pan under the firebox when the trailer is displaced lateral on curves also provides an unrestricted air opening between the ash pan and the mud ring on all four sides.

. . . One of the greatest problems in connection with the use of the limited cut-off is to provide for the increase in the main crank pin and driving box loads which results from the high initial piston load. The solution of this problem has been attacked in an original manner in the new 2-8-4.. . . The main rod is built in two parts, one of which drives directly on the main crank pin, while the other carries back part of the load to the rear crank pin, thus relieving the main crank pin of one-quarter of the full driving load.

. . . In addition to the auxiliary starting port which is regularly incorporated in the valve chamber bushings of limited maximum cut-off locomotives, the cut-off at the front end of the cylinder is increased slightly over that at the rear end at starting and very slow speeds, by lengthening two of the ports in the front valve chamber bushing.. . . This simple expedient effectively increases the period of steam admission at slow speeds, but as the speed increases the amount

General arrangement drawing of the A-1. Compare the size of the firebox with that of the 8000, as seen on p. 13. (Railway Review, *September 12, 1925.*)

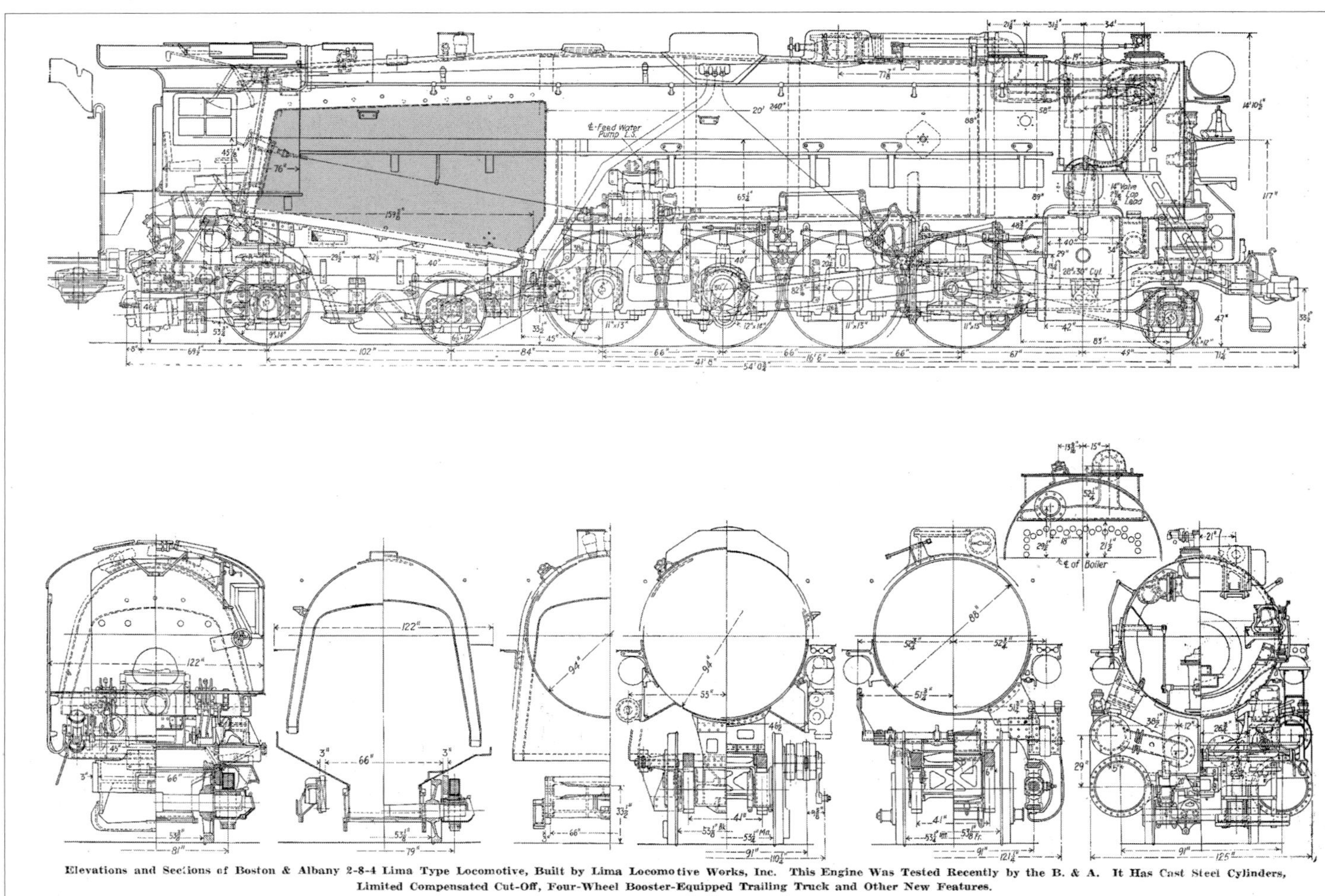

Elevations and Sections of Boston & Albany 2-8-4 Lima Type Locomotive, Built by Lima Locomotive Works, Inc. This Engine Was Tested Recently by the B. & A. It Has Cast Steel Cylinders, Limited Compensated Cut-Off, Four-Wheel Booster-Equipped Trailing Truck and Other New Features.

of steam admitted through the extension of the two ports gradually decreases until it become negligible. . . . For a nominal 60 per cent cut-off, the ports and valves are positioned to give an actual cut-off of about 60 per cent in the rear end of the cylinder and 63 per cent in the front end.

Aside from the firebox the boiler does not differ materially from the usual type. . . .Steam is taken from an outside dry pipe to the Type E superheater header at the rear of the smoke box. The throttle is located in the smoke box just ahead of the smoke stack. . . . There are two turrets from which steam is distributed to the auxiliaries. . . .

[the feedwater heater] is mounted on brackets in the front of the front end. . . ."

The Franklin booster was attached to the rear axle of the trailing truck, to give additional tractive effort for starting and at slow speeds. The tender was a NYC-design rectangular water-bottom type with 18-tons and 15,000-gallons capacity.

A smokebox view of the A-1 was fairly similar to other locomotives of its era, with the long boiler-tube/wood pilot, and brow-mounted Elesco feedwater heater, centered headlight, and front-mounted bell. The air pumps were mounted on the pilot beam and encased in shields. (Lima Photo, Kevin Kohls Collection)

The backhead of the Lima A-1 2-8-4 was cluttered with gauges and controls and dominated by the Elvin mechanical stoker apparatus. The wheel to the right is a Precision Power Reverse gear Type F. The two triangular boxes extending from the floor are the stoker elevators. (Lima Photo, Kevin Kohls Collection)

Four-Wheel Booster-Equipped Articulated Trailing Truck Used on Boston & Albany 2-8-4 Lima Type Locomotive No. 1. Articulated Connection to Main Engine Frames Is Shown at Front of Truck and Firebox Supports at Back.

*A key element in the design of the A-1 was the four wheel trailing truck, needed to support the larger firebox and grate. Some early Super Power locomotives, starting with the A-1, used the Lima Articulated Back End design, where the main frame of the locomotive ended just in front of the trailing truck, and the truck functioned as the back of the frame, including providing the mounting location for the ash pans. This design gave more room for ash pans, and saved on weight, but later experience showed that it didn't provide enough support for the back end of the boiler, while having the ash pans mounted on the truck tended to admit too much air into the firebox. Because of these problems, the use of this design fell out of favor relatively quickly. (*Railway Review, *September 12, 1925)*

Front End Showing Arrangement of Throttle Valve, Steam Pipes and Superheater and Location of Air Pumps and Feedwater Pumps

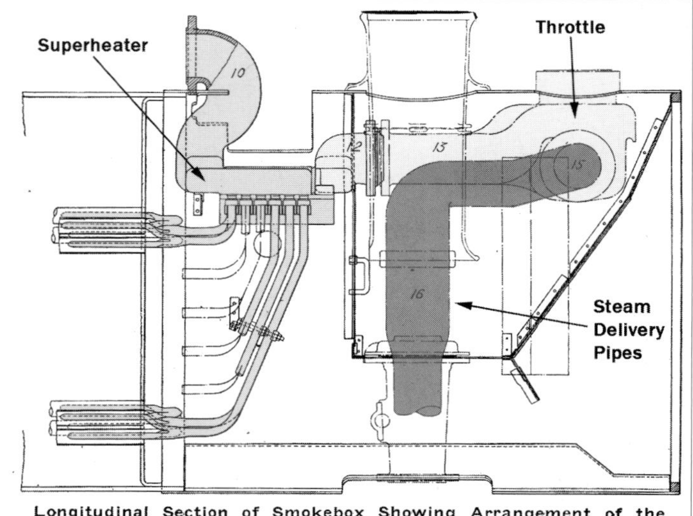

Longitudinal Section of Smokebox Showing Arrangement of the Superheater and Throttle

*Above and Above Right: these two illustrations show the arrangement of the Type E superheater and front end throttle in the smokebox. The Type E superheater differed from the earlier Type A in that the there was only one superheater element in each flue, allowing the flues to be smaller, but each element passed through two different flues. The net result was significantly more superheater surface area, and thus significantly higer superheat of the steam. (*Railway and Locomotive Engineering, *May, 1925)*

Forked Connecting Rod for Transferring Thrust Directly Back to Rear Driving Wheels

*Right: The A-1 had much higher piston thrusts than previous designs, and used the then novel "tandem main rod" to transfer some of this thrust directly to the rear driver crankpin, distributing the thrust over two crank pins and thus decreasing crank pin bearing wear. (*Railway and Locomotive Engineering, *May, 1925)*

This illustration shows how extensions were fitted to the ends of the piston valve bores, allowing external exhaust pipes to route spent steam to the exhaust ports at the center of the cylinder saddle. (Railway Review, *September 12, 1925)*

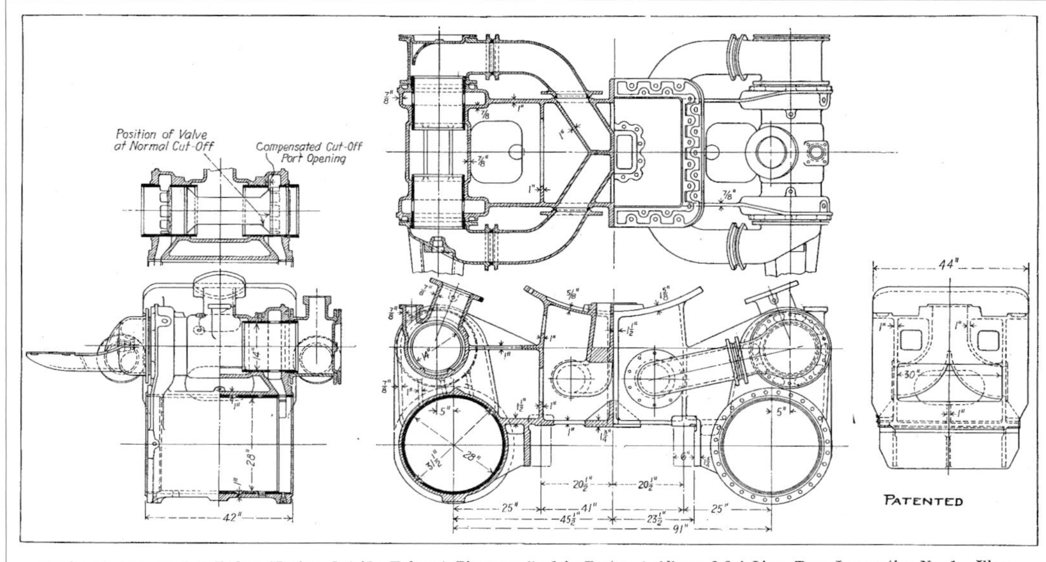

Details of Cast Steel Cylinders Having Outside Exhaust Pipes as Used in Boston & Albany 2-8-4 Lima Type Locomotive No. 1. Illustration Shows Valve Chamber Arrangement Used With Limited Compensated Cut-Off. These Cylinders Weigh 4,000 Pounds Less Than Cast Iron Cylinders of Similar Construction.

Cast Steel Cylinders Used on Boston & Albany 2-8-4 Lima Type Locomotive, Showing Arrangement of Valve Chamber Extensions, Outside Steam Pipes and Connection for Smoke Box, Steam Pipes, Relief Valves, and Exhaust Steam Pipes to Feed Water Heater.

The complete cylinder assembly. The exhaust ports at the center of the cylinder saddle are clearly visible, as are the external exhaust pipes leading from each end of the valve chambers. The large openings at the center of each valve are the main steam admission ports, flanked by smaller ports for relief valves. The small ports on the valve extensions at the top of the photo provide exhaust steam to the feedwater heater. (Railway Review, *September 12, 1925)*

This illustration shows how the main rod end was forked and enclosed the front of the side rod leading to the rear driver, and how these two rods shared a common bushing. This arrangement was called a "tandem main rod" and allowed the transfer of some of the piston thrust directly to the rear driver's crank pin, distributing the load across two crank pins rather than one. This design became a standard feature on virtually all Super Power locomotives. (Railway and Locomotive Engineering, *May, 1925)*

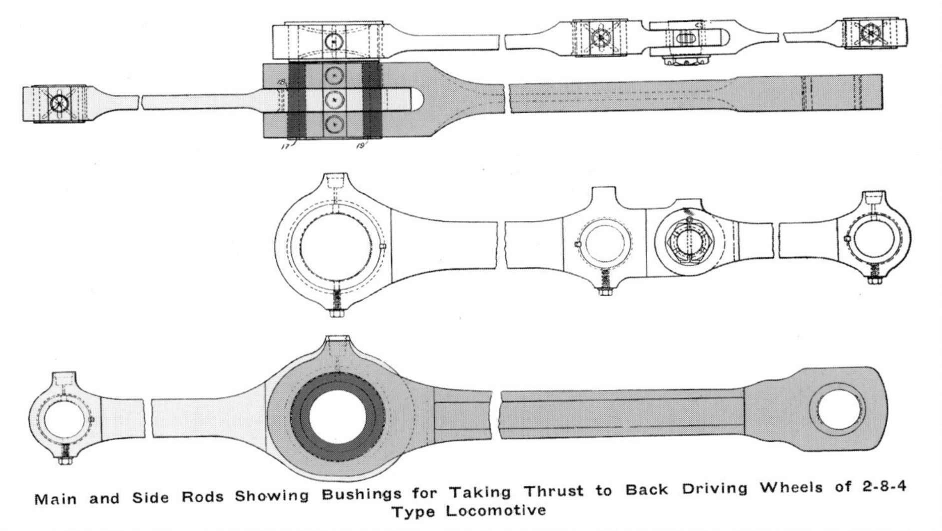

Main and Side Rods Showing Bushings for Taking Thrust to Back Driving Wheels of 2-8-4 Type Locomotive

Testing the A-1

The A-1 test was done in regular train service on NYC subsidiary Boston & Albany beginning Feb. 28, 1925, on the Albany Division between Selkirk and Washington, New York. A report was written by F. A. Butler, NYC Superintendent of Motive Power & Rolling Stock. The article reproduced numerous diagrams, indicator cards, tables, and data about the extensive tests by NYC dynamometer car X-8006 and its technical crew. The following diagram showing the test run of April 14th is reproduced below, along with Mr. Butler's comments:

Note that both engines ran the same route on the same day, nearly simultaneously. The 190 took 3 hours 15 minutes to cover the 46.3 miles, hauling 1691 tons. The A-1 took 2 hours 18 minutes (29% less time, or 41% faster) to haul 2296 tons (36% more) the same distance. A common way of evaluating the performance of a freight locomotive is to look at the Gross Ton-Miles per Train Hour, which is proportional to the average drawbar horsepower of the locomotive. In this case, the 190 generated 24,090 GTM/TH, where the A-1 generated 46,219 GTM/TH, 92% more, or nearly double what the already quite capable H-10 class 190 produced. The new design concepts embodied on the A-1 were certainly vindicated.

"On this day Mikado engine No. 190 started from Selkirk with a manifest train of 46 cars, 1,691 tons 47, minutes ahead of 2-8-4 type class A-1 which had 54 cars, 2,296 tons. Both trains ran without delays, the A-1 overtaking the no. 190 at a point shown on the diagram. At Chatham No. 190 took the outside track so that at the time of passing the two trains were running side by side on parallel tracks under exactly the same conditions. Between East Chatham and Canaan is a difficult part of the line, with many curves and a heavy grade, the severity of this part of the line in comparison with other sections having similar average grade conditions not being adequately shown by the condensed profile [in the diagram].

This run may be taken as a fair comparison of the relative ability of the two engines to move freight over the line. The uniform speed of the 2-8-4 type locomotive over the test division is noteworthy as indicated by the uniform slope of the time curve.

The following data compiled from the test results of the two locomotives is a comparison on the basis of gross ton-miles and fuel.

Average Dynamometer Horsepower, Which is Proportional to Ton-Miles per Hour

Fired per hour	A-1 (HP)	Mikado (HP)	Per cent increase A-1 Average lb. dry coal over Mikado
4,000	1,200	+	--
4,500	1,350	+	--
5,000	1,480	1,200	23.5
5,500	1,600	1,250	28
6,000	1,750	1,320	33
6,500	*	1,420	--
7,000	*	1,550	--
7,500	*	1,650	--

* The A-1 never reached these rates of firing.
+ The Mikado never ran at as low rates as these during the test.

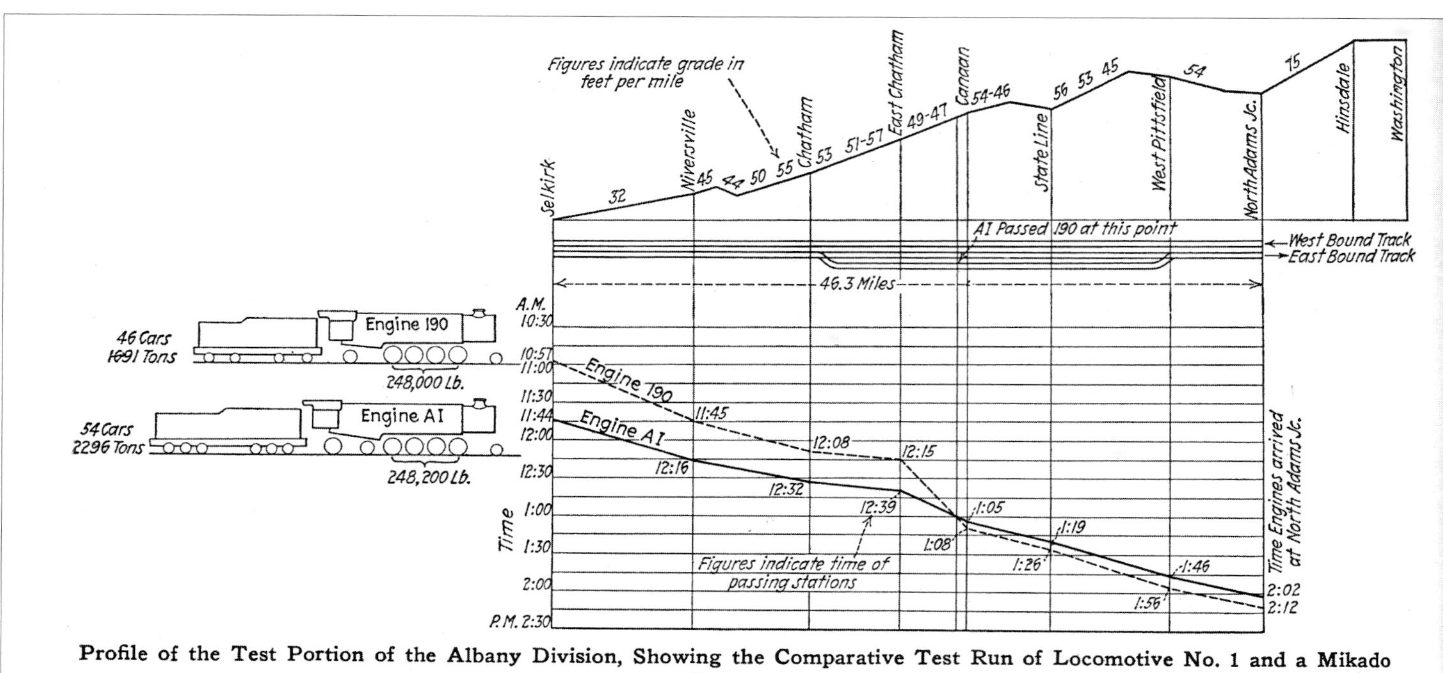

Profile of the Test Portion of the Albany Division, Showing the Comparative Test Run of Locomotive No. 1 and a Mikado Locomotive

. . . Trials were run to determine the best point of cut-off consistent with prompt starting under the worst conditions of rail, grade and position of the cranks. It was found that 60 per cent maximum cut-off best met this condition. With this cut-off an indicated tractive force of 69,400 lb. was obtained at slow speeds. The indicator cards gave a very even turning moment with the result that with this tractive force, giving a factor of 3.58, there was no more tendency to slip than there would be with a full stroke cut-off engine. . . Prompt starting was secured under all conditions. . . .

No trouble was developed with the new type of rod drive . . . No hot pins or main boxes trouble developed, although with 240 lb. pressure the piston thrust is 148,000 lb. . . . Indicating the correctness of the theory that this rod drive distributes the thrust over two pairs of wheels.

No trouble of any kind was experienced with the tracking or operation of the articulated trailing truck . . . Particular comment is made upon the large ash pan and the ease with which it can be dumped. . ."

In the next issue of the magazine, an editorial comment stated the following: ". . . It [the test] clearly shows the meaning of horsepower, the importance of which as applied to the transportation of freight is becoming increasingly evident with the growing need for better utilization both of motive power and roadway facilities. . ." The editorial went on to comment about how important the demonstrated decrease in fuel consumption coupled with the increase of ton-miles per train hour was highly significant for future locomotive design.

LIMA LOCOMOTIVE WORKS CLASS A-1 NO. 1 ORDER NO. 1070									
DELIVERED	FEBRUARY, 1925					CONSTRUCTION NUMBERS		6883	
WHEEL ARRANGEMENT	DRIVING WHEEL DIAMETER		CYLINDERS		BOILER		FIREBOX		
2-8-4	63"		DIAMETER	STROKE	DIAMETER	PRESSURE	LENGTH	WIDTH	GRATE AREA
			28"	30"	88 1/16"	240 p.s.i.	150 1/8"	96¼"	100 SQ.FT.
WHEEL BASE			TRACTIVE POWER		FACTOR OF ADHESION		TUBES AND FLUES		
DRIVING	ENGINE	ENGINE AND TENDER	MAIN CYLINDERS WITH BOOSTER				NUMBER	DIAMETER	LENGTH
16' 6"	41' 8"	82' 6"	69,400 lbs. 82,600 lbs.		3.58		90 204	2¼" 3½"	20' 0"
AVERAGE WEIGHT IN WORKING ORDER, POUNDS					HEATING SURFACES, SQUARE FEET				
ON DRIVERS	TRUCK	TRAILER		TOTAL ENGINE	TUBES AND FLUES	FIREBOX	ARCH TUBES	TOTAL	SUPERHEATER
		FRONT AXLE	REAR AXLE						
248,200	35,500	48,400	52,900	385,000	4,773	284	53	5,110	2,111
TENDER									
TYPE	FUEL	WATER	WEIGHT, FULLY LOADED						
12 WHEEL	18 TONS	15,000 GALS	275,000 LBS.						

*The A-1 crossing the Selkirk Bridge just east of Albany, N.Y. with a test train during its test period on the Boston & Albany. The box-like structure on the pilot is a shelter for the test engineers who rode the pilot, taking measurements using instrumentation installed in the valves and cylinders. (*Railway Age*, September 12, 1925)*

B. & A. Locomotive No. 1 Leaving the Selkirk Bridge

The A-1 with a dynamometer car and test train on the Albany Division of the Boston & Albany. (Railway Review, *September 12, 1925)*

B&A eventually received 55 of the new 2-8-4s from Lima and proceeded to name them "Berkshire" after the mountains that dominated the line's heaviest grades, a name which was almost universally used on other lines as well (with the notable exception of the 90 operated by C&O which called them "Kanawha" instead and the 25 belonging to the Missouri Pacific, which called them "Limas").

At about this same time Alco and NYC were designing a new locomotive as well, one that would use some of the design features used on the A-1, and this would result in the line's large fleet of 4-8-2 Mountain types.

In July of 1925 the A-1 tested on the Chesapeake & Ohio's Alleghany Subdivision between Clifton Forge, Virginia, and Hinton, West Virginia, hauling both coal and fast freight trains. Though C&O was impressed with the test results, it did not order any of the new types because it felt that the recently received Class K-3 heavy 2-8-2s were almost as good for this service, and the new Class H-7 simple articulated 2-8-8-2s were better for the heavy coal trains. But, in later years C&O would be one of Lima's best customers.

The A-1 then went on to test on the Illinois Central, Milwaukee Road, and Missouri Pacific. The IC was impressed and ordered 50 2-8-4s that were virtually the same as the A-1 sample. It too broke from the Berkshire name and called them "Limas." The Missouri Pacific purchased 25 of the new type, while Milwaukee Road declined to order any.

After all the testing, the A-1 returned to Lima for refurbishing, and then was sold to the IC, were it remained in service until being retired and scrapped in 1955. It is certainly too bad that a locomotive of such epochal importance was not saved.

With the successful tests of the A-1, Lima had proven that a new concept in design was possible and feasible. It began advertising the new locomotives as "Super Power," a name/slogan it would use to the very end of its steam building. It was a stroke of public relations genius, as it captured the spirit of the new age of railroading that the engines introduced and fostered. Other builders would construct similar locomotives, and all are equally deserving of the appellation of Super Power, but only Lima used it at the time.

In the next 34 years Lima would build 699 locomotives that fit the Super Power mold, each one having a particular character. And, over this time the basic design features of the concept continued to be refined and improved. The balance of this book will be devoted to examining in a summary fashion and illustrating each of these locomotive types. No attempt is being made to construct a detailed history of each type on each railroad that bought them, but to show an overall picture of the entire fleet as it was distributed over the continent on the Class I railroads that became Lima's customers for locomotives of this design.

Of course, Lima didn't concentrate all its efforts just on Super Power, but continued to build locomotives of all types for both domestic and foreign use, as well as its Shays.

During its test period on the Boston & Albany, the A-1 was lettered for that road. After the test period was completed the engine returned to Lima for a mechanical check-up before it left again to demonstrate on other roads. For this purpose, the tender was relettered for the Lima Locomotive Works, as shown in this photo of the engine with some of the shop crew who worked on it. (Allen County Historical Society Collection)

The A-1 during its demonstration period on the Milwaukee Road. If you look closely you can see that the Milwaukee replaced the A-1's tender with one of their own. (Allen County Historical Society Collection)

The A-1 is seen here testing on the Illinois Central. Unlike on the Cheapeake & Ohio and the Milwaukee road, both of which tested the A-1 but did not buy any examples of its kind, the Illinois Central bought 50 copies, and then later the A-1 itself. (Allen County Historical Society Collection)

How to Define Super Power

Gene Huddleston, writing in *Chesapeake & Ohio Super Power*, published by the C&O Historical Society in 2005 which is by far the best book devoted to this type of modern locomotive on any railroad in the United States, noted:

> "A too easy definition of Super Power is any steam locomotive with a four wheel trailing truck. The reason for going from no trailing truck, to a two-wheel, then four-wheel, and finally a six-wheel, was to permit an ever larger firebox with grates located behind the driving wheels in order to have more firebox volume for more complete combustion. As to four wheels being the "rule," there are always exceptions, which show that it was grate area in square feet more than a four-wheel truck that defined Super Power. For example, the New York Central from 1925 to 1944 purchased several hundred of the every successful class L-2, L-3, and L-4 Mountain type (4-8-2), called Mohawks on the NYC. The firebox resting on the two-wheel trailing truck was 75.3 square feet in area, whereas the Northern Type (4-8-4) class U-4b purchased from Lima in 1938 by the Grand Truck Western, had less grate area (73.7 square feet) over its four wheel trailing truck."

This observation then raises the issue of what, exactly, constituted a Super Power locomotive. A look at the novel features of the A-1, and the 8000 before it, provides some guidance. The 8000 introduced the use of

- Hollow axles and crank pins to reduce weight;
- An external dry pipe to take steam from the boiler to the superheater header;
- The Type E superheater to provide hotter, dryer steam to the cylinders;
- A front end throttle, throttling superheat-

ed rather than saturated steam;

- The use of superheated steam in the auxiliaries (air pumps, generator, etc);
- Making the booster an integral part of the locomotive's design and operation;
- Long valve travel, with Baker valve gear;
- The use of a feedwater heater to improve overall efficiency.

To this the A-1 added

- A much larger firebox, with a correspondingly larger grate, to support more efficient combustion of the fuel;
- A four wheel trailing truck to support the weight of the larger firebox;
- Making the trailing truck an integral part of the locomotive's frame, articulated from the back end of the frame itself and containing the drawbar connection to the tender;
- The use of limited cut-off to decrease the use of steam when starting;
- Higher boiler pressure, compensating for the loss of tractive effort when starting due to the limited cut-off, and providing higher boiler efficiency overall;
- Tandem main rods, which distribute the force from the pistons onto both the driven axle and the one behind it.

Together, these two locomotives pioneered the set of features which defined the early Super Power locomotive.

As time passed, and experience was gained, this feature set evolved, and certain of these features were discarded in favor of other concepts. The relatively small 63" drivers of the 8000 and the A-1 were found to be too small to allow adequate counterbalancing and the new standard became 69" for most freight locomotives. The use of a combustion chamber to increase the furnace volume became standard (it's absence in both the 8000 and the A-1 is quite curious, since the earlier USRA designs included it), and then it was no longer necessary to have such a large grate just to provide a large furnace volume, so later 2-8-4s tended to have grates of 90 sq. ft., as compared to the A-1's 100. The outside dry pipe proved to be unnecessary, and didn't appear on any but the earliest Super Power locomotives. The articulated back end proved to be troublesome, and was replaced by a conventional four wheel Delta trailing truck. Finally, the limited cut-off feature never gained in popularity, and many roads which bought locomotives with this feature modified them to full cut-off later. So, a later Super Power locomotive could have been defined as a locomotive that had the following features:

- A large furnace volume, comprised of both the firebox and a large combustion chamber ahead of the firebox;
- A large grate, but not quite so large as in years past;
- A four wheel Delta trailing truck supporting the large firebox;
- High boiler pressure;
- The Type E superheater with integral front end throttle;
- A high efficiency feedwater heater;
- Drivers sufficiently large as to allow adequate counterbalancing at road speeds, rather than drag speeds .

A number of features were found on many, if not most, Super Power locomotives, were omitted from some locomotives that were clearly Super Power, Most notable among these were the booster and Baker valve gear.

Some have argued that a true Super Power locomotive had its firebox completely behind the driving wheels, with the grates below the tops of the drivers. With the exception of the Allegheny type (2-6-6-6) and the N&W Class A (2-6-6-4), all Super Power articulated locomotives – Challengers (4-6-6-4), Big Boys (4-8-8-4), and Yellowstones (2-8-8-4) – violated this "rule", yet were undoubtedly still Super Power locomotives.

Finally, even the four wheel trailing truck, as Gene Huddleston noted, is not a sure indicator of a Super Power locomotive. The NYC Mohawks (4-8-2) of the L3 and L4 classes are arguably Super Power locomotives, despite their wheel arrangement. The L4a produced a cylinder horsepower of 5,400, some 65% more than the A-1, and a drawbar horsepower of nearly 4,300. Another locomotive whose wheel arrangement, and in this case cylinder arrangement, would argue against membership in the Super Power club was N&W's magnificent Y-6b compound 2-8-8-2s. These locomotives were capable of 5,600 drawbar HP, clearly indicating that these were, in fact, Super Power locomotives.

Lima was constantly involved in advertising its products and especially in the later years of steam in pushing the idea of the continued economy, and efficiency of modern steam against diesels. Since it was the smallest of the builders, its management may have felt as well the need to keep its name in front of railroad managers especially with ads in Railway Age, Railway Mechanical Engineer, and other trade magazines.

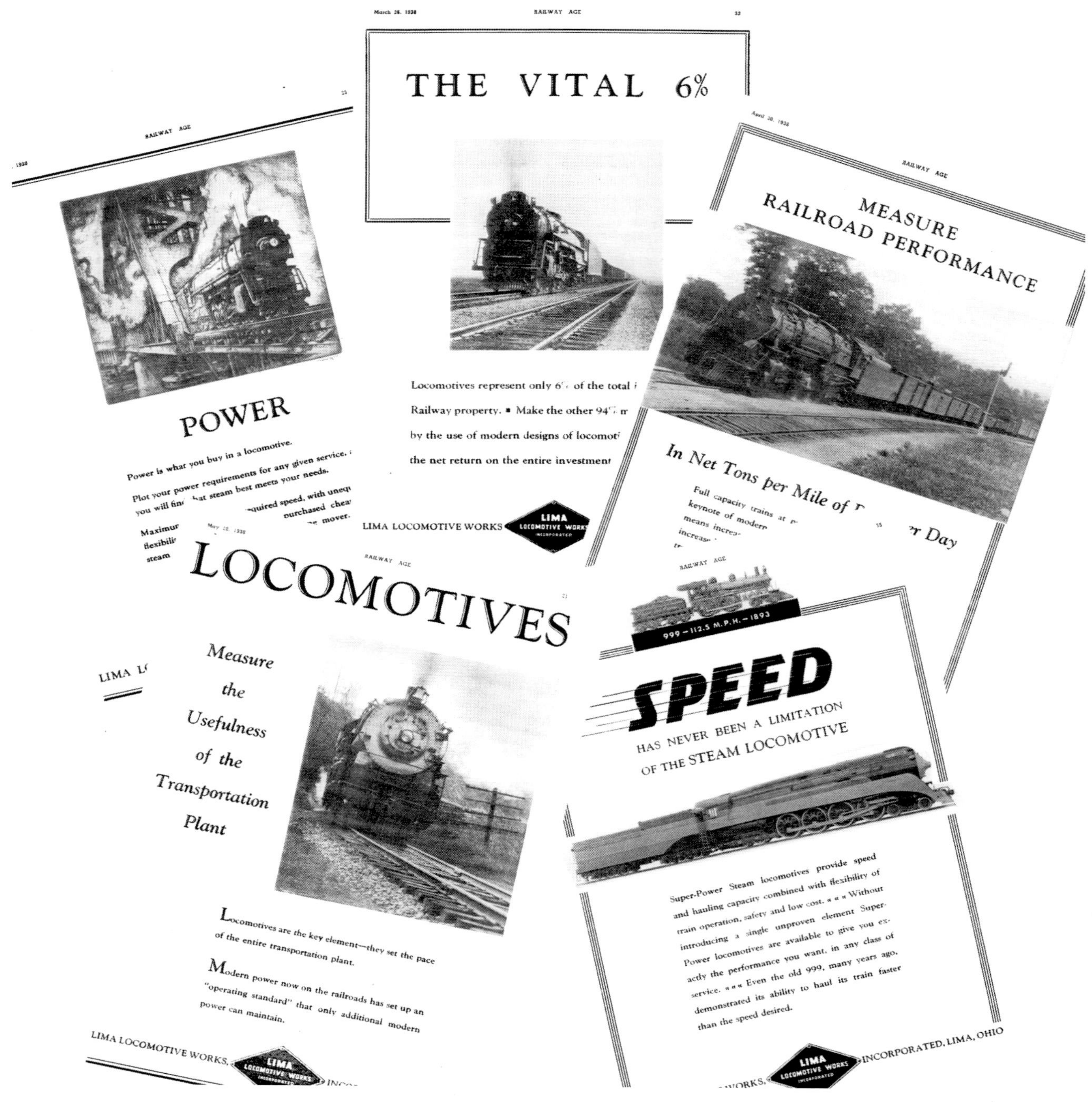

Railroad	Wheel Arrangement	Date Built	Road Nos.
Lima Loco Works (Later IC)	2-8-4	2/1925	A-1
Texas & Pacific	2-10-4	11-12/1925	600-610
	2-10-4	6/1927	611-624
	2-10-4	2-3/1928	625-639
	2-10-4	6-7/1928	640-654
	2-10-4	11-12/1929	655-669
Illinois Central	2-8-4	10-12/1926	7000-7049
Boston & Albany	2-8-4	2-3/1926	1400-1424
	2-8-4	12/1926	1425-1444
	2-8-4	8/1930	1445-1454
	4-6-4	4-5/1931	610-619
Erie	2-8-4	9-10/1927	3325-3349
	2-8-4	8-9/1929	3385-3404
Boston & Maine	2-8-4	5/1928	4000-4019
	2-8-4	9/1929	4020-4024
NYC & St. L. (NKP)	4-6-4	11/1929	174-177
	2-8-4	6-7/1942	715-729
	2-8-4	3-5/1943	730-739
	2-8-4	1-3/1944	740-754
	2-8-4	8-9/1944	755-769
	2-8-4	3-5/1949	770-779
Missouri Pacific	2-8-4	5-7/1930	1901-1925
Chicago Great Western	2-10-4	4/1930	850-864
	2-10-4	12/1930	880-885
Chesapeake & Ohio	2-10-4	9-11/1930	3000-3039
	4-8-4	12/1935	600-604
	2-6-6-6	12/41-1/42	1600-1609
	4-8-4	1/1942	605-606
	2-6-6-6	9-10/1942	1610-1619
	2-6-6-6	7-8/1944	1620-1629
	2-6-6-6	10-12/1944	1630-1644
	2-8-4	9-12/1945	2740-2749
	2-8-4	1-3/1947	2750-2759
	4-8-4	6/1948	610-614
	2-6-6-6	12/1948	1645-1659
Detroit, Toledo & Ironton	2-8-4	12/1935	700-703
	2-8-4	12/1939	704-705
Southern Pacific	4-8-4	12/1936	4410-4415
	4-8-4	10-12/1937	4416-4429
	2-8-8-4	10-11/1938	3800-3811
	4-8-4	3-5/1939	4430-4449
	4-8-4	3-6/1942	4450-4459
	4-8-4	7-8/1943	4460-4463
	4-8-4	8/1943	4464-4469
Pere Marquette	2-8-4	9-11/1937	1201-1215
	2-8-4	10-11/1941	1216-1227
	2-8-4	3-5/1941	1228-1239
Wisconsin Central (Soo Line)	4-8-4	1/1938	5000-5003
Grand Trunk Western	4-8-4	7-8/1938	6405-6409
Kansas City Southern	2-10-4	7-9/1937	905-909
Western Pacific	4-8-4	6-7/1943	481-486
Richmond, Fredericksburg & Potomac	2-8-4	1-3/1943	571-580
Central of Georgia	4-8-4	8-10/1943	451-458
Virginian	2-6-6-6	3-6/1944	900-907
	2-8-4	6-7/1946	505-509
Louisville & Nashville	2-8-4	1-5/1949	1970-1991

In an impressive action photo, I-1b No. 628, one of 70 Lima 2-10-4s on the railroad, has an oil train in tow at Weatherwood, Texas, in February 1948. T&P was heavily involved in the Texas oil boom of the 1920s-30s. (Philip H. Leroy Photo, Jay Williams Collection)

One would expect that the first order for Super Power locomotives that Lima built would be of the pioneering 2-8-4 type, but that wasn't the case. The first Super Power order came from the Texas & Pacific Railway for another entirely new wheel arrangement, the 2-10-4, which the company called "Texas Type," a name which was forever after applied to 2-10-4s wherever they operated.

The T&P operated entirely within Texas and Louisiana, its main line running between El Paso and New Orleans, with other lines reaching Texarkana and Sherman. Up until the discovery of oil at Ranger, Texas, in 1918, T&P was a fairly poor regional carrier, but the income from the post-1918 oil boom allowed the company to completely rehabilitate and improve itself. Missouri Pacific began buying interest in T&P in the 1920s and by 1930 controlled the company. T&P operated in close association with MoPac, although it was not merged into that company until 1976.

By 1920 T&P's motive power consisted of some old locomotives of various types and a group of 2-10-2 Santa Fe types purchased from Baldwin 1916-1919, and Mikados from the same period. However, by the mid-1920s with the oil boom in full stride, T&P management realized that new power was needed. Conveniently, Lima had just produced the 2-8-4 prototype, which had been given a great deal of fanfare in the trade press, and had tested on various roads, including the Missouri Pacific.

We have no records as to why T&P decided to go to Lima, since its experience with its earlier motive power was mostly with Baldwin, but it might be inferred that the characteristics that Lima was reporting for its new design were the deciding factor. T&P wanted a powerful locomotive that could carry trains at reasonably fast speeds to handle the oil business itself and all the other freight that was being generated by the economic boom in the region. It had been considering articulateds, but when the A-1 tests on various railroads were so widely reported, T&P officials seem to have decided to come to Lima for a solution.

We are also left to wonder why the entirely new wheel arrangement of 2-10-4 was decided upon. A ten-coupled locomotive was familiar to T&P since the mainstay of its fleet was the 2-10-2 type, and apparently this arrangement was pleasing to the T&P management from the standpoint of weight on each axle.

When T&P and Lima mechanical engineers finalized the design, the product was not too much different from the Lima A-1 2-8-4 in power, weight, boiler dimensions, etc., but just added an extra set of driving wheels and lengthened the boiler. Other changes from the Berkshire were,

TEXAS & PACIFIC CLASS I-1 NO. 600-609 ORDER NO. 1080									
DELIVERED	600-608: NOVEMBER, 1925; 609-610: DECEMBER, 1925					CONSTRUCTION NUMBERS		6959-6968	
WHEEL ARRANGEMENT	DRIVING WHEEL DIAMETER		CYLINDERS		BOILER		FIREBOX		
2-10-4	63"		DIAMETER	STROKE	DIAMETER	PRESSURE	LENGTH	WIDTH	GRATE AREA
			29"	32"	86½"	250 p.s.i.	150 ⅛"	96¼"	100 SQ.FT.
WHEEL BASE			TRACTIVE POWER		FACTOR OF ADHESION		TUBES AND FLUES		
DRIVING	ENGINE	ENGINE AND TENDER	MAIN CYLINDERS WITH BOOSTER				NUMBER	DIAMETER	LENGTH
22' 0"	46' 8"	86' 8"	83,000 lbs. 96,000 lbs.		3.62		82 184	2¼" 3½"	21' 6"
AVERAGE WEIGHT IN WORKING ORDER, POUNDS					HEATING SURFACES, SQUARE FEET				
ON DRIVERS	TRUCK	TRAILER		TOTAL ENGINE	TUBES AND FLUES	FIREBOX & COMB. CHAM.	SYPHONS	TOTAL	SUPERHEATER
300,000	41,800	106,200		448,000	4,640	375	98	5,113	2,100
TENDER									
TYPE	FUEL	WATER	WEIGHT, FULLY LOADED						
12 WHEEL	5,000 GALS OIL	14,000 GALS	277,200 LBS.						

of course, made.

The first order was for 10 locomotives, and they were delivered in November and December 1925, making them the first Super Power to be built after the debut of the A-1. T&P eventually came back to Lima for four additional orders, so that by 1929 it had 70 of the type in operation, more than any other class on the line. In fact, the last 30 years of T&P steam is largely the story of the 2-10-4s. The T&P assigned class I-1 to the first class of new engines. Subsequent classes were I-1 a, b, c, and d.

An article that appeared in the December 19, 1925 issue of *Railway Age* described the new T&P locomotives, and did a comparison between the 2-10-4s and the Lima 2-8-4. The article has this comparison of major dimensions between the A-1 and the T&P 2-10-4s:

	T&P 2-10-4	Lima A-1
Cylinders, diameter & stroke	29x32 in.	28x30 in.
Cut-off, in full gear	60 %	60 %
Boiler pressure	250 psi	240 psi
Weights in Working Order		
On Drivers	300,000 lbs.	248,200 lbs.
Front Truck	41,800 lbs.	35,500 lbs.
Rear Truck	106,200 lbs.	101,300 lbs.
Total Engine	448,000 lbs.	385,000 lbs.
Diameter of Drivers	63 in.	63 in.
Heating Surfaces		
Firebox and Combustion Chamber	473 sq. ft.	337 sq. ft.
Tubes & flues	4,640 sq. ft.	4,773 sq. ft.
Total evaporating	5,113 sq. ft.	5,110 sq. ft.
Superheater	2,100 sq. ft.	2,111 sq. ft.
Total, Heating Surface Combined	7,213 sq. ft.	7,221 sq. ft.
Grate Area	100 sq. ft.	100 sq. ft.
Rated Tractive Power		
Engine	83,000 lbs.	69,400 lbs.
Engine & Booster	96,000 lbs.	82,600 lbs.
Factor of Adhesion	3.62	3.58

As can be seen from the table, the 2-10-4s exerted about 26% more tractive effort than the 2-8-4, had essentially the same heating surfaces, and weighed about 15% more. Because the additional weight on drivers was distributed over five instead of four axles, the loading was about 2,000 pounds less than on the 2-8-4.

The difference in the boiler came in the way that the heating surface was distributed. The tubes and flues of the Texas were about 1-½ feet longer, but fewer in number. For the I-1 the ratio of firebox heating surface to total heating surface was 6.6% for the A-1 and 9.26 % for the I-1, which by Cole's ratio gave the it 10 % more evaporating capacity. The actual increase in surface in the firebox was 39 %.

The boiler on the 2-10-4 was longer because of the additional wheel base, and allowed for a 42-inch combustion chamber. Unlike the A-1, which had its steam dome pushed well forward and had an outside dry pipe, the I-1 had the dome moved back above the combustion chamber and had an internal dry pipe. The cylinders featured a cast external pipe that carried exhaust steam which was bolted onto the cylinder. This saved 4,000 pounds in weight over conventional cylinders.

The 2-10-4s did have an articulated trailing truck similar to the A-1's. Both had articulated driving rods. Tenders had a capacity of 5,000 gal-

TEXAS & PACIFIC CLASS I-1A NO. 610-624 ORDER NO. 1101			
DELIVERED	610-624: JUNE, 1927	CONSTRUCTION NUMBERS	7237-7251

TEXAS & PACIFIC CLASS I-1B NO. 625-639 ORDER NO. 1104			
DELIVERED	625-634: FEBRUARY, 1928; 635-639: MARCH, 1928	CONSTRUCTION NUMBERS	7297-7311

TEXAS & PACIFIC CLASS I-1C NO. 640-654 ORDER NO. 1106			
DELIVERED	640-651: JUNE, 1928; 652-654: JULY, 1928	CONSTRUCTION NUMBERS	7314-7328

TEXAS & PACIFIC CLASS I-1D NO. 655-669 ORDER NO. 1116			
DELIVERED	655: NOVEMBER, 1929; 656-669: DECEMBER, 1929	CONSTRUCTION NUMBERS	7428-7442

lons of oil fuel and 14,000 gallons of water, this being one of the few Super Power types that used oil fuel. The Tractive effort of the main cylinders showed an increase of 19%.

The first new 2-10-4s were assigned initially to a run on the T&P's Ft. Worth and Rio Grande divisions between Marshall and Big Springs, Texas, a distance of 450 miles with ruling grades of 1.5 % of six miles and eleven miles in length, with heavy curvature. The booster was specifically applied for use on these grades.

The first order of the I-1 class showed they could handle 44 % more tonnage at 42 % less fuel, and did it in 33 % less time. Performance was so satisfactory that subsequent orders came quickly and by late 1929 T&P had 70 of these locomotives. These results were so spectacular that the Super Power concept was firmly established as an important part of the future of locomotive design in the United States.

It is interesting to note that the 70 T&P Texas types were in total number the largest single class of Super Power built by Lima for any railroad.

Below: Lima builders photo of I-1b No. 637. The appearance of the T&P 2-10-4s was as a long, slender engine, because the boiler and cab didn't quite fit the later really big, compact Super Power look. (Lima photo, Allen County Historical Society Collection)

I-1b No. 635 is shown here in left side view. T&P numbered its locomotives very boldly with huge numerals on the cab, yet had a sedate Roman road name on the tender side. No. 635 is at Ft. Worth March 2, 1948, toward the end of its long productive life. Note that at some point a second angular sandbox has been added to the boiler top just in front of the cab. (F. E. Ardrey, Jr. Photo, Jay Williams Collection)

Much as the Berkshire type became the dominant locomotive on the NKP, B&A, and Erie, the 2-10-4 dominated the T&P.

As with most railroads, dieselization came fairly quickly to T&P, with F7s starting in 1949 and 1950 followed by GP7s from1950 to 1957. The 2-10-4s were out of service quickly and were all scrapped except No. 610 which was placed on display at the Southwestern Stock Exposition. In 1976 it was refurbished and used on the American Freedom Train, and for a few years afterward the Southern Railway used it in excursion work.

Lima's smokebox view of No. 610 shows the impressive front end with the glowering Elesco feed water heater, slightly off-center smoke box door and headlight/number board, shielded air pumps, and heavy slatted pilot. This was certainly an impressive face! The arrangement is reminiscent of the Lima A-1. (Lima Photo, Kevin Kohls Collection)

T&P 2-10-4 is undergoing rebuilding at Marshall, Texas, with disc drivers and roller bearings on the trailing truck. (Jay Williams Collection)

No. 664, a member of the I-1d class, the last of the T&P Texas types, is on a fast freight at Ft. Worth, March 1940. Note the second sand box just behind the steam dome, apparently added by the railroad. (S. C. Van Winkle Photo, TLC Collection)

Opposite Bottom: This slightly elevated view shows I-1a No. 619 to good advantage. The usually tall, boxy sandbox was a distinguishing feature of these locomotives. Not nearly as "clean" in appearance as most later Super Power, they had a maze of piping and devices. No. 619 is about to take an extra freight out of Longview, Texas in 1935. (Jay Williams collection)

No. 666, an I-1d is at Longview, Texas, March 10, 1937, not quite a decade into its work as one of T&P's mainstay locomotive types. One can easily see the oil tank in the tender in the space normally occupied by coal. The flared stack is another distinctive characteristic of these locomotives. Like No. 664, above, this engine has a round second sandbox behind the steam dome. (Jay Williams Collection)

Manifest freight train XB2 is headed east on "Englishman's Curve" at East Chatham, New York with B&A 2-8-4 No. 1423 in charge April 11, 1932 during a light rain. (Rail Photo Service, TLC Collection)

There is hardly a railroad that is more closely associated with Lima Super Power than the Boston & Albany. This is because the A-1 2-8-4 first tested on this road, with its tender lettered not for Lima but for B&A. But, more importantly the new wheel 2-8-4 arrangement was named for B&A's own Berkshire mountains over which the first tests of the A-1 were conducted and widely reported in the railroad trade press. The tests are described at page 20 of this book.

B&A was the first to order 2-8-4s, beating Illinois Central by a few months. The first 25 came in early 1926, followed by 20 more a year later, and 10 in mid-1930. B&A also bought one other Lima Super Power locomotive type, the 4-6-4 Hudson, of which 10 were delivered in early 1931. Interestingly enough B&A assigned a class designation for the new locomotives as A-1a, followed by A-1b and A-1c for the later two orders. They were given road numbers 1400-1454.

B&A was one of about a dozen railroads that were leased by New York Central and existed as separate companies, yet operationally were integrated into the over-arching New York Central Lines. B&A had been under NYC lease since about 1900.

B&A essentially was an east-west line across Massachusetts connecting Boston with NYC at Albany, New York, with a few branches reaching other towns in Massachusetts. In the western reaches of the state the line encountered the Berkshires, and it was over the grades here that the Lima A-1 was first tested, and then the subsequent copies supplied to B&A were run throughout their lives.

Up to this time B&A was forwarding its traffic on a fairly slow ("drag era") basis using heavy 2-8-0s and medium 2-8-2s as well as a dozen or so 2-6-6-2 compound articulated types. By the time all 55 Berkshires were in service, the entire main line was being powered largely by these workhorses. The net result was a remarkable increase in speed and tonnage, as the older locomotives were soon relegated to lesser duties. H. W. Pontin, long-time B&A fireman and engineer who later ran Rail Photo Service (responsible for

These two builder broadsides of No. 1400 give a full appreciation of the type. Compare with the broadside photo of Lima's prototype A-1 on page 4 and it is easily seen that the design and appearance are almost identical, right down to the prominent feature of the outside dry pipe. (Lima Photos, Kevin Kohls Collection)

many of the great late steam-era photos of American railroads that exist today) gave Richard J. Cook his memories in Cook's *Lima Super Steam Locomotives* book in 1966 (that book served as the inspiration for this volume) and said that trips from Boston to Springfield, a hundred miles, often took 14 hours with the old locomotives, and the road was always clogged with traffic, but once the 2-8-4s arrived this was remedied very quickly and the same trip then took only about four hours. He says ". . . for sheer get up and go, the A-1-C was really brilliant. Naturally they got all the fast freight carded runs right off, and at that time, the Boston & Albany had about eight each way on each division within the 24-hour period."

Apparently after WWII some or all of the 2-8-4s had their boiler pressure dropped to 200 pounds and the 60% cut-off feature eliminated. As with all other steam, they were edged out by the arrival of diesels after the war, ending service in the early 1950s.

The other Super Power locomotives B&A acquired from Lima were ten 4-6-4 Hudson types, B&A Class J-2c, road numbers 610-619. These locomotives arrived in early 1931. They were the last locomotives Lima delivered for nearly three years as the Depression closed its plant for lack of orders.

The NYC was, after all, the originator of the 4-6-4 wheel arrangement, and named it the "Hudson Type," yet Lima built only these ten for subsidiary B&A, as against 275 built by Alco for NYC and its other subsidiaries.

These fine looking locomotives operated the best of the passenger trains between Boston and Albany without change throughout their lives, with great efficiency and lack of maintenance issues, until NYC Mohawks began to run through off the NYC at Albany. Like the Berkshires, the Hudsons were eventually modified to a lower boiler pressure of 200 psi and to eliminate the 60% cut-off. Now almost a footnote in locomotive history as the B&A's Super Power memories are almost all about the great Berkshires, the Hudsons were nonetheless great locomotives which did a superior job for two decades before falling to the all-conquering diesels.

BOSTON & ALBANY CLASS A-1a NO. 1400-1424 ORDER NO. 1082

DELIVERED	1400-1413: FEBRUARY, 1926; 1414-1424: MARCH, 1926	CONSTRUCTION NUMBERS	6979-7003

WHEEL ARRANGEMENT	DRIVING WHEEL DIAMETER	CYLINDERS		BOILER		FIREBOX		
		DIAMETER	STROKE	DIAMETER	PRESSURE	LENGTH	WIDTH	GRATE AREA
2-8-4	63"	28"	30"	88"	240 p.s.i.	150 1/8"	96¼"	100 SQ.FT.

WHEEL BASE			TRACTIVE POWER	FACTOR OF ADHESION		TUBES AND FLUES		
DRIVING	ENGINE	ENGINE AND TENDER	MAIN CYLINDERS WITH BOOSTER			NUMBER	DIAMETER	LENGTH
16' 6"	41' 8"	75' 8½"	69,400 lbs. 81,400 lbs.	3.6		90 204	2¼" 3½"	20' 0"

AVERAGE WEIGHT IN WORKING ORDER, POUNDS					HEATING SURFACES, SQUARE FEET				
ON DRIVERS	TRUCK	TRAILER		TOTAL ENGINE	TUBES AND FLUES	FIREBOX & COMB. CHAM.	SYPHONS	TOTAL	SUPERHEATER
		FRONT AXLE	REAR AXLE						
249,500	36,000	49,500	54,000	389,000	4,773	284	53	5,110	2,111

TENDER			
TYPE	FUEL	WATER	WEIGHT, FULLY LOADED
8 WHEEL	16 TONS	10,000 GALS	201,900 LBS.

NOTE: Dimensions are given for the A-1a class of 1926, most of which remained constant in the A-1b, and A-1c classes in the next two years. The major changes were that the increase in weights on drivers and trailing trucks, which increased the overall engine weight from 389,000 pounds or the A-1a to 390,500 for the A-1b, and 396,100 for the A-1c. Rated tractive power, boiler and furnace dimensions, and grate area remained the same. With the increase in weights the factor of adhesion changed from 3.6 in the A-1a and A-1b to 3.64 in the A-1c. Tender capacity on the A-1c was raised from 16 tons and 10,000 gallons to 21 tons and 15,500 gallons giving them tenders more in keeping with those usually assigned to Super Power locomotives. Other changes included the feedwater heaters and the elimination of the external dry pipe.

BOSTON & ALBANY CLASS A-1b NO. 1425-1444 ORDER NO. 1095

DELIVERED	1425-1444: DECEMBER, 1926	CONSTRUCTION NUMBERS	7192-7211

BOSTON & ALBANY CLASS A-1c NO. 1445-1454 ORDER NO. 1123

DELIVERED	1445-1454: AUGUST, 1930	CONSTRUCTION NUMBERS	7556-7565

A Lima in-construction photo taken from the cab looking forward shows the top of a B&A 2-8-4 as it was being put together on the Lima erecting floor. Closest to the camera is the cab roof, then two steam turrets in boxes, the generator, three safety valves in a casing, inspection cover, big sand box, steam dome, and just visible at left dry pipe. The big pipe on left is to convey superheated steam to the turrets. (Lima Photo, Kevin Kohls Collection)

Another top view, after completion, shows a B&A Berkshire's prominent exterior dry pipe leading from the forward-placed steam dome. The big boxy sandbox is right behind. (Lima Photo, Kevin Kohls Collection)

A great action view has A-1a 1407 leading on a doubleheaded WWII-era fast freight between Springfield and Selkirk in May 1942. The A-1a had an enlarged sand box. (Ray Curl Photo, Jay Williams Collection)

Unlike A-1a and A-1b classes the A-1c had among the cleanest faces of any Super Power Steam, No. 1448 is seen in this head-on builder's photo. Unlike many Super Power steam locomotives, the bell is not placed in the front, but the air pumps are, in the shields that would be more or less a standard for the Lima Super Power units. Similarly the Elesco feedwater brow of the earlier B&A 2-8-4s is replaced by a Coffin feedwater heater in the smokebox. (Lima photo, Kevin Kohls Collection)

Opposite Top: A-1c No. 1452 with light graphite-paint on its smokebox poses at Boson Park, Massachusetts, May 21, 1939. Minus the outside dry pipe, brow-mounted Elesco feedwater heater and with a different type of trailing truck, these locomotives presented a much different appearance than the earlier B&A Berkshires, though they were just two years later in production. (Jay Williams collection)

With a westbound empty oil train at Weston Park, Mass., in October 1942, A-1c No. 1445 poses for this NYC official photo. (Jay Williams Collection)

BOSTON & ALBANY CLASS J-2c NO. 610-619 ORDER NO. 1126									
DELIVERED	610-611: APRIL, 1931; 612-619: MAY, 1931					CONSTRUCTION NUMBERS		7574-7583	
WHEEL ARRANGEMENT	DRIVING WHEEL DIAMETER		CYLINDERS		BOILER		FIREBOX		
			DIAMETER	STROKE	DIAMETER	PRESSURE	LENGTH	WIDTH	GRATE AREA
4-6-4	75"		25"	28"	84¼"	240 p.s.i.	130"	96¼"	100 SQ.FT.
WHEEL BASE			TRACTIVE POWER		FACTOR OF ADHESION		TUBES AND FLUES		
DRIVING	ENGINE	ENGINE AND TENDER	MAIN CYLINDERS WITH BOOSTER				NUMBER	DIAMETER	LENGTH
14' 0"	40' 4"	76' 1½"	44,800 lbs. 55,400 lbs.		4.20		37 201	2¼" 3½"	20' 6"
AVERAGE WEIGHT IN WORKING ORDER, POUNDS					HEATING SURFACES, SQUARE FEET				
ON DRIVERS	TRUCK	TRAILER		TOTAL ENGINE	TUBES AND FLUES	FIREBOX & COMB. CHAM.	ARCH TUBES	TOTAL	SUPERHEATER
		FRONT AXLE	REAR AXLE						
188,100	67,100	46,500	55,300	389,000	4,203	244	37	4,484	1,920
TENDER									
TYPE	FUEL	WATER	WEIGHT, FULLY LOADED						
8 WHEEL	17 TONS	10,000 GALS	201,900 LBS.						

Builder broadside of J-2c Hudson Type No. 610 illustrates its clean lines, and high 75-inch drivers to good effect. The small tender seems a little incongruous for a Super Power locomotive, though. (Lima Photo, Kevin Kohls Collection)

Hudson No. 618 is at Boston in 1935, waiting assignment to a name passenger train for the west. (Jay Williams collection)

The Illinois Central ordered Super Power locomotives only once from Lima, a group of 50 Berkshires, but it also has the distinction of having purchased the famous Lima A-1 test locomotive as well.

The IC operated a high-class main line of over 900 miles extending almost directly north-south between Chicago and New Orleans. It had a maze of other lines as well, one of which reached as far west as Omaha and eastward as far as Louisville and Birmingham. Calling itself the "Mainline of Mid-America," it really was that as far as north-south operation was concerned. Railroads largely followed the pattern of American migration, running east-west. Only a few were built on a north-south axis (notably the SAL and ACL along the eastern Seaboard, IC in the center of the country, and some of SP's lines along the west coast).

In the 20th Century IC got its first heavy freight locomotives in 1911 with delivery of Baldwin 2-8-2s, and they soon became the backbone of the IC motive power fleet. Though this same era saw the introduction and large-scale acceptance of the compound articulated design, IC really had no mountainous regions that would require this type, so it never bought any new. It did eventually roster ten 2-6-6-2s secondhand from Central of Georgia. Lima built 97 of the Mikado types for IC in 1915-16, fifty more in 1918 and yet more in 1923, so IC had a good relationship with Lima and was very well pleased with its products.

A batch of 68 2-10-2s for IC in 1921 made Lima's locomotives among the most numerous in the IC mainline freight motive power roster.

During the testing of Lima's A-1 2-8-4, it operated on the Illinois Central, and very favorably impressed the road's motive power officials, who seem to have been partial to Lima products already. The A-1 pitted against the IC's 2-10-2s bested them by impressive margins: On average the A-1 hauled almost 300 tons more per train, maintained an average speed of 3 miles per hour more, and averaged 12,110 more gross tons per train hour than the 2-10-2s. Coal used by the A-1 as compared with the Santa Fe types was about 40% less. These were unmistakable advantages of the new concept over the old.

In June 1926 IC placed an order for fifty 2-8-4s with Lima which would complement its fleet of recent 2-8-2s and 2-10-2s. The dimensions of these locomotives were similar to the A-1. They-could be considered an almost exact copy in all major dimensions from boilers and firebox size, weight, wheelbase and diameter, and heating surface The tractive effort was exactly the same, though there was a slight variance in the tractive power with booster of an additional 1,000 pounds

ILLINIOS CENTRAL NO. 7000-7049 (LATER 8000-8049) ORDER NO. 1093

DELIVERED	CONSTRUCTION NUMBERS
7000-7014: OCTOBER, 1926; 7015-7038: NOVEMBER, 1926; 7039-7049: DECEMBER, 1926	7136-7185

WHEEL ARRANGEMENT	DRIVING WHEEL DIAMETER	CYLINDERS DIAMETER	CYLINDERS STROKE	BOILER DIAMETER	BOILER PRESSURE	FIREBOX LENGTH	FIREBOX WIDTH	FIREBOX GRATE AREA
2-8-4	63"	28"	30"	88"	240 p.s.i.	150 1/8"	96¼"	100 SQ.FT.

WHEEL BASE DRIVING	WHEEL BASE ENGINE	WHEEL BASE ENGINE AND TENDER	TRACTIVE POWER MAIN CYLINDERS WITH BOOSTER	FACTOR OF ADHESION		TUBES AND FLUES NUMBER	TUBES AND FLUES DIAMETER	TUBES AND FLUES LENGTH
16' 6"	41' 8"	99' 5 ¾"	69,400 lbs. 81,400 lbs.	3.57		88 204	2¼" 3½"	20' 0"

AVERAGE WEIGHT IN WORKING ORDER, POUNDS: ON DRIVERS	TRUCK	TRAILER FRONT AXLE	TRAILER REAR AXLE	TOTAL ENGINE	HEATING SURFACES, SQUARE FEET: TUBES AND FLUES	FIREBOX & COMB. CHAM.	SYPHONS	TOTAL	SUPERHEATER
248,000	35,000	50,000	55,000	388,000	4,750	284	130	5,164	2,111

TENDER: TYPE	FUEL	WATER	WEIGHT, FULLY LOADED
12 WHEEL	20 TONS	15,000 GALS	286,000 LBS.

ALL WERE REBUILT WITH 1 INCH SMALLER BORE CYLINDERS AND RAISED BOILER PRESSURE TO 265 PSI IN 1939 AND GIVEN NEW NUMBERS, EXCEPT NO. 7038, WHICH WAS REBUILT AS A 4-6-4 UNDER NUMBER 1. LIMA A-1, WHICH WAS NO. 7050, WAS ALSO REBUILT AND BECAME 8050.

Aside from the Worthington feedwater heater replacing the Elesco unit, this Lima broadside photo of IC 7049 looks almost exactly the same as the Lima A-1, right down to the forward steam dome with the outside dry pipe. (Lima Locomotive Works photo, Allen County Historical Society collection)

The IC Berkshires had an impressive appearance, as this right side photo shows, with the Elesco feedwater heater up front and the aggregation of plumbing around the boiler. The front-mounted bell was imitative, as so much else, of the Lima A-1. No. 7024 is at Centralia, Illinois, Dec. 5, 1934. (R. J. Foster Photo, Jay Williams Collection)

Left side view of the first of the IC 2-8-4s, No. 7000, at St. Louis, Illinois, April 9,1934, showing the big steam dome with its exterior dry pipe. This was a common European design but wasn't often used in the U. S. Lima used it on the A-1 and a few other engines, but it was not popular and didn't persist in Super Power design. (R. J. Foster photo, Jay Williams Collection)

for the IC locomotives. The IC 2-8-4s were numbered 7000-7049. One variance between the IC engines and the A-1 is that the last 10 IC engines were equipped with a Worthington type BL feedwater heater, unlike the A-1 and IC 7000—7039, which were equipped with Elesco feedwater heaters.

Because the two locomotives were so close in dimension, one could imagine that the IC simply ordered copies of the A-1 without doing any extensive study of exacting needs as did many other railroads. At any rate, the IC was a road that didn't face particular topographical challenges that might have required a more specialized look at the dimensions required. It seems as though the A-1's tests were so satisfactory the IC simply said to duplicate it.

Indeed, the A-1 fit so well into the fleet that when Lima was finished with it as a demonstrator, the IC purchased it November 20, 1927 and added it to the end of the series as 7050.

The 2-8-4s were often used on trains operating between Centralia and Cairo, Illinois, through the hilly southern Illinois country (part of the Ozarks), where grades of up to 0.75 % were encountered along with considerable curvature. They performed well and allowed elimination of helper locomotives in this area. They also handled the fast, overnight LCL and through manifest freight trains between Chicago and St. Louis with considerable success.

However, after a few years of service IC found that the Berkshires had problems, among which was that they were very rough riders at higher speeds. This resulted in several locomotives braking driving rods and engine frames.

Another problem was that the articulated trailing truck, identical to the A-1s design, would derail when backing trains. It will be remembered that the tractive force of the engine was transmitted to the tender and train through this type of trailing truck, rather than through a draw-bar attached to the locomotive frame. The company was also less than satisfied with the amount of time and money that had to be spent in repair and maintenance given the young age of the 2-8-4s. In 1939, after 15 years of service, they were taken into IC's famous Paducah, Kentucky, shops and rebuilt. The rebuilt locomotives were given new numbers 8000-8049. One, No. 7038, was rebuilt as a 4-6-4 Hudson for use in fast, light freight train work mainly in forwarding LCL freight on expedited schedules. This wasn't un-

IC 7041 has a different look because of its Worthington feedwater heater strapped to the left side rather than the up-front Elesco. The absence of the Elesco heater gives a better impression of the boiler's size and renders the clean face that was characteristic of Super Power overall. (TLC Collection)

usual since IC bought no new commercially-built steam after 1929, contenting itself with either rebuilding existing locomotives, or building its own from scratch.

During the rebuilds, the Berkshire cylinders were reduced by one inch in diameter and the boiler pressure raised by 15 psi.

Dieselization came to the IC in the early 1950s with purchases of EMD GP7s and GP9s through 1957. Mainline steam was gradually replaced over this period, with as much work as possible being squeezed out of the steam because of IC's aggressive rebuilding program (over 400 locomotives.) Most could be considered no more than a decade old.

IC is one road where Lima Super Power didn't get a "rave review."

Another photo at East St. Louis in October 1934, this time shows 7044 with its Worthington feedwater heater under the running board, and the clean face with high-mounted bell, centered headlight and up front pumps. However, unlike most Lima Super Power designs the pumps are not shielded. Half of the IC order had Worthington and half had Elesco feed water heaters. The hump ahead of the stack is the throttle. (R. J. Foster Photo, Jay Williams Collection)

No. 8020 is a rebuilt version of the IC's 2-8-4. The first impression is a much less cluttered boiler and firebox, because the feedwater heater and booster have been removed. Other changes include a set of disc drivers and solid engine truck wheels added. (TLC Collection)

Boston & Maine was a fairly early buyer of Super Power Berkshires from Lima, acquiring 20 in 1928 and five more in 1929. They were given class T-1 and road numbers 4000-4024.

Boston & Maine had lines radiating from Boston north into New Hampshire, the lower edge of Maine at Portland, east-west through Massachusetts into the edge of eastern New York state at Mechanicsville, and north-south through the center of Connecticut. It had a long grade but fairly easy ascent for eastbound from Mechanicsville to Boston, rising at .3 percent to Hoosac Tunnel. The steepest grade was one percent from Boston to Fitchburg. Otherwise its operations were not greatly affected by difficult topography.

B&M freights were handled mainly by Consolidation type 2-8-0s, as well as 2-6-0 Moguls. In fact B&M had one of the largest fleet of this generally underused wheel arrangement. It also tried four 2-6-6-2s in 1910 as the compound type was first being introduced to American railroads, but never bought any more. Between 1920 and 1923 B&M acquired bigger power in the form on 2-10-2 Santa Fe types, but these were more geared to the drag-era traffic than to the need for speed that came to the fore in the mid-1920s.

By the mid-1920s customers were demanding faster speed for their freight as the modern era of industrialization and business got into high gear, so B&M looked for something new. At this time the Lima A-1 made its epochal tests on nearby Boston & Albany, and in the following couple of years B&M officials were able to observe the huge difference the B&A Berkshires made in completely revolutionizing that road's traffic, and B&M decided to try out the 2-8-4s. It ordered 20 of the type in 1928, and added five more the following year. They were very close in design and dimensions to the Lima A-1 and to the B&A 2-8-4s.

One very visible difference was the Coffin feedwater heater which was mounted externally on top of the smokebox, giving the locomotives a very distinctive look on the front end. On the B&M they weren't called Berkshires but rather "Limas."

Although most users of Lima Super Power were highly pleased with their locomotives, it is apparent that B&M wasn't entirely satisfied with the "Limas." They were slippery, so B&M reduced the cylinder diameter a small amount and added weight on the drivers to help solve this, and yet the 2-8-4s didn't get the glowing reviews that many Super Power locomotives were receiving by the 1920s and 1930s on numerous roads. The 63-inch drivers on the T-1s were also a problem as B&M tried to increase the speed of its manifest freight trains. This was a lesson learned late at Lima, that a higher driver was re-

BOSTON & MAINE CLASS T-1A NO. 4000-4019 ORDER NO. 1103										
DELIVERED		4000-4019: MAY, 1928					CONSTRUCTION NUMBERS		7277-7296	
WHEEL ARRANGEMENT		DRIVING WHEEL DIAMETER		CYLINDERS		BOILER		FIREBOX		
				DIAMETER	STROKE	DIAMETER	PRESSURE	LENGTH	WIDTH	GRATE AREA
2-8-4		63"		28"	30"	88"	240 p.s.i.	150 ⅛"	96¼"	100 SQ.FT.
WHEEL BASE				TRACTIVE POWER		FACTOR OF ADHESION		TUBES AND FLUES		
DRIVING	ENGINE		ENGINE AND TENDER	MAIN CYLINDERS WITH BOOSTER				NUMBER	DIAMETER	LENGTH
16' 6"	41' 8"		80' 3¾"	69,400 lbs. 81,400 lbs.		3.60		86 204	2¼" 3½"	20' 0"
AVERAGE WEIGHT IN WORKING ORDER, POUNDS						HEATING SURFACES, SQUARE FEET				
ON DRIVERS	TRUCK		TRAILER FRONT AXLE	TRAILER REAR AXLE	TOTAL ENGINE	TUBES AND FLUES	FIREBOX & COMB. CHAM.	SYPHONS	TOTAL	SUPERHEATER
250,200	38,800		50,200	53,800	393,000	4,726	284	121	5,131	2,111
TENDER										
TYPE	FUEL		WATER	WEIGHT, FULLY LOADED						
8 WHEEL	18 TONS		12,000 GALS	216,400 LBS.						

Lima builder's photo of B&M T-1a No. 4000. Prominently visible here are the Coffin feedwater heater on the smokebox front, the early front end throttle on top of the smokebox, with the booster exhaust just behind it, both in front of the stack, and the Lima articulated back-end trailing truck. (Lima Locomotive Works photo, Allen County Historical Society collection)

Head-on, the B&M 2-8-4s had a very unusual look because of the curving Coffin Feedwater heater. The headlight was mounted low because mounting it on the smokebox door would have prevented the door opening fully because of the feedwater heater. The bell also found its location here, along with shielded pumps. The front end throttle is at the top of the view and the whistle is just seen to the right. (Lima Photo, Kevin Kohls Collection)

No. 4001 in broadside at Boston in 1935. (W. R. Osborne Photo, TLC Collection)

ally needed for its Super Power engines.

Eventually, in the late 1930s, B&M got five high-drivered (73-inch) 4-8-2 Mountain types from Baldwin, which helped with the fast freights. After the glut of WWII traffic when everything that the motive power department could provide was in constant use, including some leased locomotives, B&M started buying diesels and very quickly (in 1945) sold ten of the 2-8-4s to power-hungry Santa Fe and the other ten to Southern Pacific. These were the only Lima Super Power types ever to operate for second owners. Santa Fe kept some looking just as they did on the B&M, but some had their bulky Coffin feedwater heater replaced, so their appearance changed, and they were converted to oil fuel. The B&M Limas are among the most distinguishable Super Power types because of the Coffin heater.

BOSTON & MAINE CLASS T-1B NO. 4020-4024 ORDER NO. 1112										
DELIVERED		4020-4024: SEPTEMBER, 1929					CONSTRUCTION NUMBERS		7374-7378	
WHEEL ARRANGEMENT		DRIVING WHEEL DIAMETER		CYLINDERS		BOILER		FIREBOX		
				DIAMETER	STROKE	DIAMETER	PRESSURE	LENGTH	WIDTH	GRATE AREA
2-8-4		63"		28"	30"	88"	240 p.s.i.	150 1/8"	96¼"	100 SQ.FT.
WHEEL BASE				TRACTIVE POWER		FACTOR OF ADHESION		TUBES AND FLUES		
DRIVING	ENGINE		ENGINE AND TENDER	MAIN CYLINDERS WITH BOOSTER				NUMBER	DIAMETER	LENGTH
16' 6"	41' 8"		80' 3¾"	69,400 lbs. 81,400 lbs.		3.60		86 204	2¼" 3½"	20' 0"
AVERAGE WEIGHT IN WORKING ORDER, POUNDS						HEATING SURFACES, SQUARE FEET				
ON DRIVERS	TRUCK		TRAILER		TOTAL ENGINE	TUBES AND FLUES	FIREBOX & COMB. CHAM.	SYPHONS	TOTAL	SUPERHEATER
			FRONT AXLE	REAR AXLE						
255,800	38,800		50,200	53,800	*403,000*	4,726	284	121	5,131	2,111
TENDER										
TYPE	FUEL		WATER	WEIGHT, FULLY LOADED						
12 WHEEL	*23TONS*		*17,500 GALS*	*330,600 LBS.*						

Here is Santa Fe 3501, formerly B&M 4002, taken at Los Angeles Jan. 1, 1950. Although still sporting its outside Coffin heater, it has been converted to oil and has a typical SP oil tender behind. (G. M. Best Photo, Jay Williams Collection)

T-1a No. 4013 and 4002 2-8-4s and a 2-10-2 running light in the mid-1930s, obviously at some speed. That feedwater heater really gave the T-1s a menacing appearance! (Rail Photo Service, TLC Collection)

Santa Fe No. 4197 was B&M 4003. Rebuilt at Santa Fe's Topeka shops in June 1947, an Elesco heater has replaced the Coffin device, a new tender is evident, and the locomotive is hardly recognizable. Just out of the shop on June 10, 1947. (W. A. Gibson Photo, Jay Williams Collection)

Missouri Pacific consisted of a maze of lines in the states of Missouri, Arkansas, Louisiana, Texas, Oklahoma, Kansas, and Nebraska, with connections at Chicago to the north, St. Louis, Memphis, and New Orleans in the east, and Pueblo (Colorado), Omaha, and El Paso on the west.

It was in 1930 just at the onset of the Depression that Missouri Pacific ordered a single series of 2-8-4s from Lima. The 25 locomotives, given road numbers 1901-1925, were the only Lima Super Power locomotives that MP would ever buy.

In February and March of 1927 Missouri Pacific used the Lima A-1 in road tests, pitting it against recently acquired three-cylinder Mikados. This was also the era when the three-cylinder design was being contemplated as a boost to power, speed, and efficiency.

Apparently pleased with the results of these tests, MP placed a small order of five locomotives from Alco's Schenectady Works in 1928, similar in design to the Lima A-1. Although Lima developed/created/invented the Super Power concept there was noting propriety about most of it. It was more a concept of how to integrate and use to best advantage elements of locomotive construction that were commonly practiced by all the commercial builders of the era. The five Alco 2-8-4s were lettered for MP and assigned to subsidiary International-Great Northern.

Satisfied with the performance of the I-GN 2-8-4s, MP went directly to Lima for its own order of 25.

The new Lima 2-8-4s were very close in major proportions to the original Lima A-1 Berkshire (and to the Alco 2-8-4s of the I-GN). Some differences include the smaller grate area of 88.3 square feet vs. 100 and the factor of adhesion at 3.97 vs. 3.58 on the A-1. [The theoretical target which was considered best for traction was 4.0.] All of the Lima 2-8-4s built up until the MP order had boosters, but the MP did not order them. It stuck with the 63-inch drivers that the A-1 prototype had, and the tractive power rating was the same.

The MP locomotives did not use the articulated trailing truck, but had conventional connections and full-length frames. The MP locomotives also had two sand domes to provide plenty of traction at both ends of the driver set, with the steam dome positioned between them.

The MP 2-8-4s were initially used on the Kansas City-St. Louis main line on fast freights. One of the few grades that caused MP some operational concern was that from St. Louis west to Kirkwood, as the line climbed away from the Mississippi River. When the 2-8-4s arrived, they could handle a heavier train over this grade, and a much heavier train west of there, than the previously used locomotives. Because of this, to al-

MISSOURI PACIFIC CLASS BK-63 NO. 1901-1925 ORDER NO. 1120									
DELIVERED	1901-1908: MAY, 1930; 1909-1921: JUNE, 1930; 1922-1925: JULY, 1930					CONSTRUCTION NUMBERS		7476-7500	
WHEEL ARRANGEMENT	DRIVING WHEEL DIAMETER		CYLINDERS		BOILER		FIREBOX		
			DIAMETER	STROKE	DIAMETER	PRESSURE	LENGTH	WIDTH	GRATE AREA
2-8-4	63"		28"	30"	87 15/16"	240 p.s.i.	132 1/8"	96¼"	88.3 SQ.FT.
WHEEL BASE			TRACTIVE POWER		FACTOR OF ADHESION		TUBES AND FLUES		
DRIVING	ENGINE	ENGINE AND TENDER	MAIN CYLINDERS				NUMBER	DIAMETER	LENGTH
16' 9"	40' 5"	85' 0¾"	69,400 lbs.		3.97		84 204	2¼" 3½"	20' 0"
AVERAGE WEIGHT IN WORKING ORDER, POUNDS					HEATING SURFACES, SQUARE FEET				
ON DRIVERS	TRUCK	TRAILER		TOTAL ENGINE	TUBES AND FLUES	FIREBOX & COMB. CHAM.	SYPHONS	TOTAL	SUPERHEATER
		FRONT AXLE	REAR AXLE						
275,500	39,800	39,900	57,000	412,200	5,057	256	100.5	5,413	2,330
TENDER									
TYPE	FUEL	WATER	WEIGHT, FULLY LOADED						
12 WHEEL	20 TONS	17,250 GALS	321,700 LBS.						

Lima builder's photo of Missouri Pacific 2-8-4 No. 1909, showing the Worthington type BL feedwater heater mounted on the left side of the locomotive. (Lima Locomotive Works photo, Allen County Historical Society Collection)

No. 1925 is seen here St. Louis just before its conversion to a 4-8-4, having been in service for a bit over a decade. Note the two sand domes with encased pipes leading to the drivers, front and rear. The front has the clean Lima Super Power look with centered headlight and high bell, and shielded pumps on the pilot deck. (D. Bearse Photo, Jay Williams Collection)

A left side view of No. 1922 shows the Worthington BL feedwater header mounted at the running board, and the big 6-wheel tender trucks to good advantage. Taken at St. Louis June 7, 1938. (Jay Williams Collection)

low the maximum train over the entire line, MP set up a helper station that provided assistance to westbound trains. A train of about 90-100 cars could be handled by a single 2-8-4 over the whole route except for the Kirkwood grade.

The 25 Lima Berks became the only Lima Super Power class that was completely rebuilt, creating effectively an entire new locomotive. The MP's shops lengthened the boilers, added a set of drivers, which were changed to 75 inches, put on cast frames, changed the boiler pressure to 250, and changed the lead trucks to four wheel units. Thus, the 2-8-4s emerged as 4-8-4s. They were intended for use in expediting war-time freight traffic. The new drivers gave them additional speed, though the tractive effort remained similar to the 2-8-4s. These new/old locomotives were numbered 2101-2125 and remained in service until displaced by diesels in the early 1950s, thus ending a unique career for this Lima type.

This right side photo taken January 15, 1938 at Jefferson City, Missouri, shows No. 1915 well covered with sand dust after having obviously made some hard trips. (Jay Williams Collection)

This is what the 2-8-4s looked like after they were rebuilt as 4-8-4s. No. 2112 is on a fast freight at Waggoner, Oklahoma, April 16, 1949. It began as No. 1920 before rebuilding at Missouri Pacific's Sedalia shops in 1941. Some interesting features are the Boxpok drivers and the obviously lengthened boiler. Otherwise, the face is altered only by the installation of a solid pilot. (D. W. Eldridge Photo, Jay Williams Collection)

No. 854 is pictured here at St. Paul, Minnesota, at the northern extremity of the CGW line on August 16, 1937. Although a virtual duplicate to the T&P 2-10-4s the locomotive looks much different just because of the absence of the big Elesco Feedwater Heater atop the smokebox. Note how the throttle linkage goes right through the sandbox to the front end throttle just behind the stack. (Jay Williams Collection)

CHICAGO GREAT WESTERN CLASS T-1 NO. 850-864 ORDER NO. 1121

DELIVERED	850-864: APRIL, 1930	CONSTRUCTION NUMBERS	7501-7515

WHEEL ARRANGEMENT	DRIVING WHEEL DIAMETER	CYLINDERS		BOILER		FIREBOX		
		DIAMETER	STROKE	DIAMETER	PRESSURE	LENGTH	WIDTH	GRATE AREA
2-10-4	63"	29"	32"	86½"	255 p.s.i.	150 1/8"	96¼"	100 SQ.FT.

WHEEL BASE			TRACTIVE POWER	FACTOR OF ADHESION		TUBES AND FLUES		
DRIVING	ENGINE	ENGINE AND TENDER	MAIN CYLINDERS WITH BOOSTER			NUMBER	DIAMETER	LENGTH
22' 0"	46' 8"	86' 8"	84,600 lbs. 97,900 lbs.	3.59		216 50	2¼" 5½"	21' 6"

AVERAGE WEIGHT IN WORKING ORDER, POUNDS					HEATING SURFACES, SQUARE FEET				
ON DRIVERS	TRUCK	TRAILER FRONT AXLE	TRAILER REAR AXLE	TOTAL ENGINE	TUBES AND FLUES	FIREBOX & COMB. CHAM.	SYPHONS	TOTAL	SUPERHEATER
304,000	41,000	57,200	58,800	461,000	4,255	375	150	4,780	1,340

TENDER			
TYPE	FUEL	WATER	WEIGHT, FULLY LOADED
12 WHEEL	25 TONS	14,000 GALS	288,500 LBS.

CHICAGO GREAT WESTERN CLASS T-1 NO. 880-885 ORDER NO. 1124

DELIVERED	850-864: DECEMBER, 1930	CONSTRUCTION NUMBERS	7566-7571
SPECIFICATIONS IDENTICAL TO ORDER NO. 1121			

Chicago Great Western operated lines centered in Iowa and Minnesota, with main lines connecting to Chicago, Kansas City, and St. Paul/ Minneapolis. An upper Midwestern carrier of fairly small dimension, its business consisted in large part of agricultural products and products of industry.

Its motive power after 1900 consisted of a large number of the fairly uncommon 2-6-2 Prairie types of small dimensions, but nonetheless capable of handling the line's traffic in the era, along with a number of 2-8-0 Consolidations. In 1910 it jumped on the new compound articulated Mallet type band wagon and received ten 2-6-6-2s from Baldwin in 1910. They were never successful and were soon rebuilt as 4-6-2s. In 1911 CGW began buying sizeable Mikados which were received through 1918 (the last ten being USRA) as well as a class of 2-10-2s in 1916.

In 1929 the road's management changed and the new group of investors hired new managers who completely revamped the railroad. The Van Sweringens of Cleveland, well known for their control of NKP, C&O, PM, and Erie, also acquired part interest in the line.

With the new administration came an order for a radically different locomotive, a 2-10-4 Texas type, from Lima in 1929. This would become the line's main locomotive for its fast and heavy freight business. Lima built 15 in early 1930 and three more late that year, while Baldwin was building another 15 the same year, and the class was finished off with three more Lima engines in 1931. Those were the last steam the CGW would buy.

Classed T-1, 2, and 3, they had road numbers in the 800-series.

The CGW 2-10-4s were very similar to those that Lima had built for the Texas & Pacific in 1925, which established the 2-10-4 wheel type, except of course the T&P engines were oil filed and the CGW's used coal. At the same time that CGW was ordering virtual duplicates of the T&P engines of four years before, Chesapeake & Ohio was bringing the 2-10-4 to its ultimate development with monstrous locomotives delivered in 1930, which were the largest non-articulated design yet built (see page 67). The CGW locomotives were not in that league.

As the dimensions given in the table in this chapter show, the CGW 2-10-4s were very much the same as the T&P locomotives (see page 21) in almost all respects. They differed in exterior appearance by the absence of the Elesco feedwater heater high on the smokebox in preference for a Coffin heater inside the smokebox, so they had a cleaner front appearance. The T-3 class (three by Lima and six by Baldwin) had a Bethlehem auxiliary engine, located on the rear truck on the tender to supply extra power as a booster. This is another example where a Lima design was built by others.

Eventually the 2-10-4s became a hallmark of CGW as they were used on mainlines leading from the major junction at Oelwein, Iowa, to Chicago, St. Paul, and down to Kansas City.

Arrival of the Texas types also allowed retirement of some of the older locomotives still on the line. The Texans shouldered the greater burden of CGW traffic until arrival of diesels in the late 1940s. By 1951 CGW's new fleet of EMD F-unit road freight diesels had retired the 2-10-4s and other diesels had finished off the rest of the road's steam roster.

700

701
701

Detroit, Toledo & Ironton

Detroit, Toledo & Ironton's main line ran north-south from Detroit, through Toledo, Lima, Springfield, Jackson, and terminated on the southern end at Ironton, Ohio. In 1920 Henry Ford bought the railroad to act as a conduit for coal from West Virginia and Kentucky to Detroit, and as an initial distribution line for finished vehicles. His control was relinquished in 1929 when the Pennroad holding company (part of the PRR financial empire) acquired it.

In 1929 DT&I was relying almost completely on Consolidations to handle its traffic. During the early 1930s, the road added heavy Consolidations, and fifteen Decapod 2-10-0s delivered in 1916 also did much of the heavy work, including coal trains. By the latter half of the decade, with the Depression easing and the automotive industry recovering, it was decided new locomotives were needed.

Part of the answer for additional power was the purchase of six 2-8-4s from Lima. It's interesting that though DT&I served Lima, this order for six Berkshires and an order for 12 Mikados are the only locomotives that the company ever bought from Lima Locomotive Works. The 2-8-4s came in a batch of four in 1935 and two more in 1939, the latter being slightly different from the first four, but essentially of the same dimensions. They were numbered 700-705 and classed R-1.

Since DT&I had no branch lines and very little business other than heavy through traffic, it didn't need either a large variety of locomotive types, nor a large quantity. The six Lima products were, therefore, an important element in its motive power stable.

Nos. 700-703 were delivered by Lima in December 1935, and the final two, No. 704-705 were received in December 1939. They were not the last steam on the road, but they were the only Super Power. The last steam locomotives purchased by the DT&I were a dozen Lima heavy Mikados built during WWII.

DT&I dieselized as quickly as it could starting in 1950, with steam ending its last service in 1955. Seventy-two GP7s and GP9s dieselized the road freights between 1951 and 1955.

Opposite Top: Lima builder's photo of DT&I No. 700, the first 2-8-4 on that road. (Allen County Hist. Soc. coll.)

Opposite Center: The crew poses for its photo with No. 701 at Flat Rock, Mi. in November, 1952. The locomotive is far from its original haunts in southern Ohio, perhaps displaced by the arrival of diesel locomotives on the road, which began two years earlier. (Walter F.J. Krawiec photo, TLC Collection)

Opposite Bottom: R-1 class 2-8-4 No. 701 is pictured here on March 9, 1941, at Springfield, Ohio, a terminal about mid-way along DT&I's north-south mainline through Ohio. The soft light allows details to stand out, including the raised metallic numerals on the cab and logo on the tender. The front of this locomotive reminds one of the NKP 2-8-4s, but Pennsylvania RR type classification lamps were used. An interesting automatic coaling machine has just filled the tender. (TLC Collection)

DETROIT, TOLEDO & IRONTON CLASS R-1 NO. 700-703 ORDER NO. 1132

DELIVERED	700-703: DECEMBER, 1935	CONSTRUCTION NUMBERS	7632-7635

WHEEL ARRANGEMENT	DRIVING WHEEL DIAMETER	CYLINDERS		BOILER		FIREBOX		
		DIAMETER	STROKE	DIAMETER	PRESSURE	LENGTH	WIDTH	GRATE AREA
2-8-4	63"	25"	30"	88"	250 p.s.i.	132 1/8"	96¼"	88.3 SQ.FT.

WHEEL BASE			TRACTIVE POWER	FACTOR OF ADHESION		TUBES AND FLUES		
DRIVING	ENGINE	ENGINE AND TENDER	MAIN CYLINDERS			NUMBER	DIAMETER	LENGTH
16' 9"	39' 3"	86' 1¼"	63,250 lbs.	3.92		77 202	2¼" 3½"	18'

AVERAGE WEIGHT IN WORKING ORDER, POUNDS					HEATING SURFACES, SQUARE FEET				
ON DRIVERS	TRUCK	TRAILER		TOTAL ENGINE	TUBES AND FLUES	FIREBOX & COMB. CHAM.	ARCH TUBES	TOTAL	SUPERHEATER
		FRONT AXLE	REAR AXLE						
248,600	53,900	46,000	63,000	411,500	4,127	318	48	4,493	1,795

TENDER			
TYPE	FUEL	WATER	WEIGHT, 2/3 LOAD
12 WHEEL	22 TONS	22,000 GALS	284,200 LBS.

DETROIT, TOLEDO & IRONTON CLASS R-1 NO. 704-705 ORDER NO. 1149									
DELIVERED		704-705: DECEMBER, 1939				CONSTRUCTION NUMBERS		7777-7778	
WHEEL ARRANGEMENT		DRIVING WHEEL DIAMETER	CYLINDERS		BOILER		FIREBOX		
2-8-4		63"	DIAMETER	STROKE	DIAMETER	PRESSURE	LENGTH	WIDTH	GRATE AREA
			25"	30"	88"	260 p.s.i.	132 ⅛"	96¼"	88.3 SQ.FT.
WHEEL BASE			TRACTIVE POWER		FACTOR OF ADHESION		TUBES AND FLUES		
DRIVING	ENGINE	ENGINE AND TENDER	MAIN CYLINDERS				NUMBER	DIAMETER	LENGTH
16' 9"	39' 3"	86' 1¼"	65,800 lbs.		3.78		77 202	2¼" 3½"	18'
AVERAGE WEIGHT IN WORKING ORDER, POUNDS					HEATING SURFACES, SQUARE FEET				
ON DRIVERS	TRUCK	TRAILER FRONT AXLE	TRAILER REAR AXLE	TOTAL ENGINE	TUBES AND FLUES	FIREBOX & COMB. CHAM.	ARCH TUBES & CIRCULATORS	TOTAL	SUPERHEATER
248,400	54,500	48,000	65,100	416,000	4,127	318	76	4,521	1,795
TENDER									
TYPE	FUEL	WATER	WEIGHT, ⅔ LOAD						
12 WHEEL	22 TONS	22,000 GALS	284,200 LBS.						

Right side of No. 701 at Springfield Dec. 26, 1938. Note the small slatted pilot, centered headlight, high bell just in front of the feedwater heater in front of the stack. The door is closed on the "vestibule" type cab which afforded better weather protection than the standard open cabs. (Jay Williams Collection)

Opposite Top: No. 704, the last of the first order of DT&I Berkshires, is at Jackson, Ohio, September 14, 1947. (Clyde E. Helms photo, TLC Collection)

Opposite Bottom: At the very end of its life No. 705, a member of the last of the R-1 class, which arrived in 1939 is seen here at Springfield on November 15, 1953. Diesels were already handling much of the traffic and all steam would be gone in two years. (Clyde E. Helms, TLC Collection)

It is important to understand that almost half of all Lima Super Power production was built for four railroads, all of which were under the financial control of the Van Sweringens of Cleveland: Nickel Plate (New York, Chicago, & St. Louis), Chesapeake & Ohio, Pere Marquette, and Erie. These railroads became the strongest proponent of Lima's work, even though they also bought Super Power locomotives from other builders.

In the early part of the Twentieth Century Cleveland real estate developers O. P. and M. J. Van Sweringen discovered that they needed certain properties and leases that here held by the New York, Chicago & St. Louis Railroad (known as the Nickel Plate and abbreviated NKP) to complete a rapid transit line essential to the success of their Shaker Heights development project. Since this company was controlled by the New York Central, whose president Alfred Smith (not the politician) was friendly to the Vans (as they were commonly called), they arranged to buy controlling interest in the NKP, and thus entered the railroad field in 1916. The NKP was at best the poor stepchild of NYC, and needed lots of rehabilitation.

The Vans soon decided that they wanted to get into the railroad business in a bigger way, and in the mid-1920s they were able to gain control of the Erie, the Chesapeake & Ohio, the Hocking Valley, and the Pere Marquette railroads. In addition to these railroads, they purchased major interests in several other lines, but it was C&O, NKP, Erie, and PM (HV was merged into C&O in 1930) to which they paid the most attention. These companies, though they remained separate, often had the same president and officers and interlocking directorates.

The Vans used John J. Bernet as their main railroad advisor and operator. He left his position as a New York Central Vice President (at the behest of Alfred Smith) to help the Vans by becoming president of the NKP. His rehabilitation of this railroad established his credentials. He was later president of the Erie, and after that was president of C&O, NKP, and PM concurrently.

Bernet was aware of the key role that appropriate motive power played in the operations and earning power of a railroad. This, of course, was near and dear to the Van Sweringens as financial manipulators of the first order.

To effect a creation of more uniform policies and plans for their group of railroads the Van Sweringen lines sent members of the management element of their mechanical departments to a central committee, which operated out of the Cleveland headquarters with a full staff, and apparently with full authority over the mechanical operations of all the constituent railroads. This group, called the Advisory Mechanical Committee (AMC) was created in 1929.

Although records are sparse, as far as can be determined, this group had the function of overseeing the mechanical design work for the four railroads. In so doing they attempted to arrive at the best design for the work that needed to be accomplished given the characteristics of the individual railroad, but at the same time to standardize as much as possible, eliminate duplicative effort, and to ensure that the best designs were adopted by each of the lines.

Of the people who were important in the AMC's operation, foremost was Alonzo G. Trumbull who held the title "Chief Mechanical Engineer." Because of his long tenure (1929 to 1947) he had the continuity of experience to have participated in all the Super Power designs developed by the Committee for Erie, C&O, NKP and PM. Cornell educated, Trumbull was Erie's Chief Mechanical Engineer from 1922 until he moved to the AMC in 1929. He is probably the one person most responsible for the designs. D. S. Ellis, the AMC's Chief Mechanical Officer (1932-1943), and W. G. Black, who was with AMC and then Vice-President of C&O, NKP, and PM all had some part, but it is apparent from research done by E. L. Huddleston that Trumbull was the "brains" of the AMC[1].

[1]Huddleston, E. L. "A. G. Trumbull, Locomotive Designer," Chesapeake & Ohio Historical Magazine, Vol. 36, No. 9, Sept, 2004.

It appears that the AMC had the most important part in the creation of the Super Power deigns on all four railways. In addition, it also had a role in refining the design overall as used by other railroads and other builders.

The genesis of the Super Power interest on the Van Sweringen roads seems to have started in the years just before creation of the AMC when Lima, Alco, and Baldwin built the S-1,2,3, and 4 classes of huge Super Power 2-8-4s for Erie. This basic design was enlarged to create the C&O T-1 2-10-4 in 1929 (built in 1930), the first locomotive for which AMC took credit. The basic concepts were then followed in development of the famous NKP 2-8-4s, C&O's 2-8-4s, PM's 2-8-4s, and the C&O's much heralded 2-6-6-6s in subsequent years, as well as the passenger Super Power 4-8-4s and 4-6-4s for C&O.

In total between 1927 and 1949 Lima built 301 Super Power locomotives for the four Van Sweringen roads, which amounts to just under a half of its entire Super Power production, so the importance of the AMC's influence on Lima's work and vice versa should be considered in any overall evaluation of the work of either. Little original documentation survives which would show the relationships or indicate how this influence was exerted in either direction, but it can be inferred that the relationship was mutually helpful in developing and building the best possible designs within the constraints of the reciprocating steam locomotive machinery.

In November 1944 some key players in the locomotive construction game posed for Lima's official photographer commemorating completion of C&O No. 1630, first in an order for 15 more Alleghenies, bringing total to 45 . A . G . Trumbull, natty in his well-fitting coat, stands on the ground fifth from left. On Trumbull's right, fourth from left, is Clyde B . Hitch of Richmond, C&O's Chief Mechanical Officer. Left of Hitch (third from left) is N . M. Trapnell, Supt . of Motive Power of Richmond . To the right of Trumbull (sixth from left) is A .H . Glass, C&O's Chief Motive Power Inspector . The AMC staff is represented by Trumbull and by Mike Donovan (third from right) . Other AMC staff are in the picture, like Ed Hauer, but the identifier helping author Tom Dixon seemed to know only these in the front row, plus (on the end at right) Dan Ellis, ice-President of. Manufacturing for Lima since leaving his AMC post in 1943 . (C&OHS Collection)

Lima builder broadside of S-4 class Erie 2-8-4 No. 3389. This final version of the Erie Berkshires had the largest tender, carrying 28 tons and 20,000 gallons. The large boiler is not all that evident in this photo, though the locomotive displays the clean lines that was the hallmark of Super Power types. (Lima Photo, TLC Collection)

ERIE RAILROAD CLASS S-2 NO. 3325-3349 ORDER NO. 1102									
DELIVERED	3325-3340: SEPTEMBER, 1927; 3341-3349: OCTOBER, 1927					CONSTRUCTION NUMBERS		7252-7276	
WHEEL ARRANGEMENT	DRIVING WHEEL DIAMETER		CYLINDERS		BOILER		FIREBOX		
2-8-4	70"		DIAMETER	STROKE	DIAMETER	PRESSURE	LENGTH	WIDTH	GRATE AREA
			28½"	32"	92"	250 p.s.i.	150 1/16"	96¼"	100 SQ.FT.
WHEEL BASE			TRACTIVE POWER		FACTOR OF ADHESION		TUBES AND FLUES		
DRIVING	ENGINE	ENGINE AND TENDER	MAIN CYLINDERS WITH BOOSTER				NUMBER	DIAMETER	LENGTH
18' 3"	44' 0"	86' 7¾"	72,000 lbs. 85,000 lbs.		3.90		50 242	2¼" 3½"	21'
AVERAGE WEIGHT IN WORKING ORDER, POUNDS					HEATING SURFACES, SQUARE FEET				
ON DRIVERS	TRUCK	TRAILER FRONT AXLE	TRAILER REAR AXLE	TOTAL ENGINE	TUBES AND FLUES	FIREBOX & COMB. CHAM.	ARCH TUBES & CIRCULATORS	TOTAL	SUPERHEATER
274,000	51,700	64,800	67,000	457,500	5,249	320	128	5,697	2,545
TENDER									
TYPE	FUEL	WATER	WEIGHT, FULLY LOADED						
12 WHEEL	24 TONS	16,500 GALS	309,000 LBS.						

ERIE RAILROAD CLASS S-4 NO. 3385-3404 ORDER NO. 1113									
DELIVERED	3385-3394: AUGUST, 1929; 3395-3404: SEPTEMBER, 1929					CONSTRUCTION NUMBERS		7379-7398	
WHEEL ARRANGEMENT	DRIVING WHEEL DIAMETER		CYLINDERS		BOILER		FIREBOX		
2-8-4	70"		DIAMETER	STROKE	DIAMETER	PRESSURE	LENGTH	WIDTH	GRATE AREA
			28½"	32"	92"	250 p.s.i.	150 1/16"	96¼"	100 SQ.FT.
WHEEL BASE			TRACTIVE POWER		FACTOR OF ADHESION		TUBES AND FLUES		
DRIVING	ENGINE	ENGINE AND TENDER	MAIN CYLINDERS WITH BOOSTER				NUMBER	DIAMETER	LENGTH
18' 3"	44' 0"	86' 7¾"	72,000 lbs. 85,000 lbs.		3.98		50 242	2¼" 3½"	21'
AVERAGE WEIGHT IN WORKING ORDER, POUNDS					HEATING SURFACES, SQUARE FEET				
ON DRIVERS	TRUCK	TRAILER FRONT AXLE	TRAILER REAR AXLE	TOTAL ENGINE	TUBES AND FLUES	FIREBOX & COMB. CHAM.	ARCH TUBES & CIRCULATORS	TOTAL	SUPERHEATER
286,500	49,000	65,200	68,100	468,800	5,249	320	128	5,697	2,545
TENDER									
TYPE	FUEL	WATER	WEIGHT, FULLY LOADED						
12 WHEEL	28 TONS	20,000 GALS	378,000 LBS.						

The Erie was an important railroad for the Van Sweringen brothers to acquire as part of their railroad empire (see page 55) especially because it was a fairly logical extension of the Nickel Plate to the east, tapping into valuable industrial regions of New York state.

Erie was an old railroad and at the time the Van Sweringens acquired it the line extended from Jersey City west to Buffalo, and on to Cleveland, Marion (Ohio), Dayton (Ohio) with connections to Cincinnati, and Chicago. The Erie had been financially weak in previous decades and by 1926 the Vans were able to buy over 50% of its stock. In January 1927, they installed John J. Bernet as president, taking him from his duties as President of the NKP, which he had held since 1916. Bernet had rehabilitated the NKP to a large degree, and when he came to Erie he brought with him W. G. Black as "Mechanical Assistant to the President." Black had been head of motive power for NKP since 1923. He would figure importantly in the development of the Erie 2-8-4 immediately after he and Bernet moved over to the road, and would also be important in the creation of NKP and C&O Super Power engines developed by the Advisory Mechanical Committee (see page 55).

Bernet and Black immediately set to work to revamp Erie operations to fit the mold that had been established on the NKP. An important part of this was the acquisition of new motive power. At this time Erie had a stable of locomotives that featured over 200 2-8-2 Mikados, 75 of the famous 2-10-0 Russian Decapods, and almost 100 2-10-2 Santa Fe types for its heavy freight work, as well as a gaggle of old 2-8-0s, and a couple of articulateds. Black and Bernet ordered 2-8-4's immediately upon taking control of the road. Although Lima had pioneered the type with its epochal A-1 just two years before, they ordered 25 of the new type first from Alco. A second group, numbering 25 came from Lima close on its heels, then a third batch numbering 35 from Baldwin, and a final series 20 from Lima in late 1929. In less than two years Bernet and Black had re-equipped Erie's primary freight trains with the very latest design in modern locomotives, and had done it from all three of the major commercial locomotive builders.

The Alco locomotives were the first to arrive, in September 1927. *Railway Age* said the following about the new arrivals in its October 22, 1927 issue:

> ". . . . Thus, the locomotives were designed with 70-inch driving wheels for attaining greater speeds than the Mikado and Santa Fe locomotives which the new engines replace. They are being placed in main line service between Marion, Ohio, and Hornell, N. Y. . . . The ruling grades eastward are 1.295 per cent between Marion and Kent, and one per cent between Kent and Meadville. Westbound the grades are one per cent between Meadville and Kent, and 1.1315 per cent between Kent and Marion. . . ."

The new locomotives had 29½x32 inch cylinders, 90-inch boiler diameter, 225 psi boiler pressure 150x96¼ inch fireboxes, grate area 100.2 square inches, and total heating and superheating surface of 8,147 sq. ft. Weight on drivers was 276,000 lbs., and total engine weight 443,000 lbs. They were given S-1 class and assigned road numbers 3300-3324.

Just weeks later in September and October, Erie's S-2 class came in from Lima (for dimensions see table accompanying this chapter). They were placed in the same service, side-by-side with the Alco 2-8-4s. A *Railway Age* article printed in the October 8, 1927 issue compares the S-2 with Lima's prototype Berkshire, the A-1 of 1925. This was natural since the 2-8-4 wheel arrangement as a type was only three years old.

These locomotives used the Lima-designed articulated ash plan that was attached to the trailing truck rather than to the mud-ring of the firebox, almost identical to the A-1 design. The article says

> ". . . The size of the firebox and boiler does not differ materially from the A-1 boiler. The diameter of the first ring has been increased by 4 in., or to 92 in. The length between the flue sheets has been increased from 20 to 21 ft. . . . It will be seen that the cylinders of the Erie 2-8-4 have been increased to 28½ inches by 32 in. and the boiler pressure increased by 10 lb. or to 250 lb. The weight on drivers has been increased 26,000 lb., or to 274,000 lb., and the total engine weight has

been increased 72,500 lb. Above that of the A-1 or a total weight of 475,000 lb. The diameter of the driving wheels has been increased from 63 in. to 70 in.

While the grate areas are the same, the outstanding difference in boiler proportions is the increase in heating surface areas. . . . The total evaporative heating surface has been increased about 11 per cent and there is a 21 per cent increase in the amount of superheating surface resulting in an increase of combined evaporative and superheating surface of about 14 per cent."

The tractive force of the main cylinders and booster combined was 85,000 lbs.

It appears that although Lima's famous A-1 had been used as the basis of the new Erie design, it had been increased in capability and size. Size was not a limitation on the Erie because much of its main line had been built when the road was on a 6-foot broad gauge standard, so clearances were no issue. Westing and Staufer point out in *Erie Power* the large dimensions of the Erie 2-8-4s: "From rail top to stack top the locomotive measured 16 feet 4-1/16 inches; centerline of the boiler from rail measured 10 feet, 8 inches, and at the dome course the boiler's outside diameter was 100 inches. As for width the locomotive hit a figure of 11 feet 2 inches."

With the Alco and Lima Berkshires in full operation, the Erie posted almost incredible improvements in statistics for the first half of 1928: 13.4% more cars moved, 10% more gross ton-miles per train, 17.4% more gross ton-miles per train-hour, and 6.1% increased operating speeds. This plus Bernet's decision to retire more than 300 obsolete locomotives, replacing them with 2-8-4s and new switchers, helped increase Erie's operating income for 1928 by 29%. These were impressive statistics for anyone watching the railroads. Bernet was doing the same thing he had done for NKP in the previous decade, but one of his most important tools was the group of new Super Power Berkshires.

During 1928 the batch of 35 similar 2-8-4s arrived from Baldwin, giving Erie Berkshires from all three major builders. Then in 1929 the final lot of 20 Berkshires arrived from Lima, and the Erie 2-8-4 fleet was complete. Indeed, the 20 Lima locomotives of 1929 were the very last new steam locomotives that Erie purchased except for 10 Baldwin 0-8-0s delivered in 1930. The Depression wasn't good to Erie, and it entered Bankruptcy on January 18, 1938. Its fleet of massive Berkshires, however, would serve through World War II and beyond until the arrival of diesels.

According to Fred Westing in *Erie Power*, some of the hardest work that the 2-8-4s did was on coal trains over a heavy grade between Carbondale and Ararat, Pa. He says that as many as three would be used as pushers on the rear of 80-100 car trains to climb the 960 feet vertically between the two points, the hardest of which was the 410 foot rise in six miles north from Carbondale. The grade wasn't sustained, and there were many variations.

Sixty-five of the 2-8-4s were still in service in 1951 as diesels gradually overtook their work, and by 1952 they were all retired.

It was these gargantuan Berkshires that served as the prototype design from which the Van Sweringens' Advisory Mechanical Committee (see page 55) designed 2-8-4s for NKP, Pere Marquette, and C&O, as well as the C&O 2-10-4 and arguably the C&O 2-6-6-6.

This is actually the S-3 class, built not by Lima but by Baldwin, placed here to show how similar the engines from the different builders looked. About the only difference one would spot immediately is the builder's plate! (Baldwin Photo, TLC Collection)

Smokebox view of an Erie S-2 shows the clean face that would become a Super Power standard: centered headlight, high bell, shielded air pumps on the pilot beam. The prodigious size of the boiler is evident in this photo. The cast brass number plate was made by the Erie's shops. (Lima Photo, Kevin Kohls Collection)

S-2 No. 3329 is eastbound on a manifest freight near Hammond, Indiana, August 19, 1950. By this time Erie is well into diesels, and it would be only a couple of years before the Berkshires were sidetracked forever. The S-2s had a great run from 1927 to 1952, and along with their compatriots are often credited with "saving a railroad." (P. Slager Photo, Jay Williams Collection)

S-2 No. 3342 is seen here at Port Jervis, New York, on May 24, 1934, showing the fireman's side, including the prominently placed Worthington BL feed water heater below the running board. Note too that a booster had been added to the front tender truck, as indicated by the side rod connecting the middle and rear axle, supplementing the booster on the engine's trailing truck. (G. M. Best photo, TLC Collection)

This nice left side view of 3344 was taken at Meadville, Pennsylvania, September 12, 1951, toward the end of its active life. Though most railroads of the era decorated their tender flanks with a simple road name, Erie chose to use its logo prominently. By this time also modifications have caused a bit more clutter of piping, and some of the drivers have been replaced with the Boxpok type. (G. Votava Photo, Jay Williams Collection)

This photo gives a very good impression of the boiler size and emphasizes the compact very efficient look of the machine. (Jay Williams Collection)

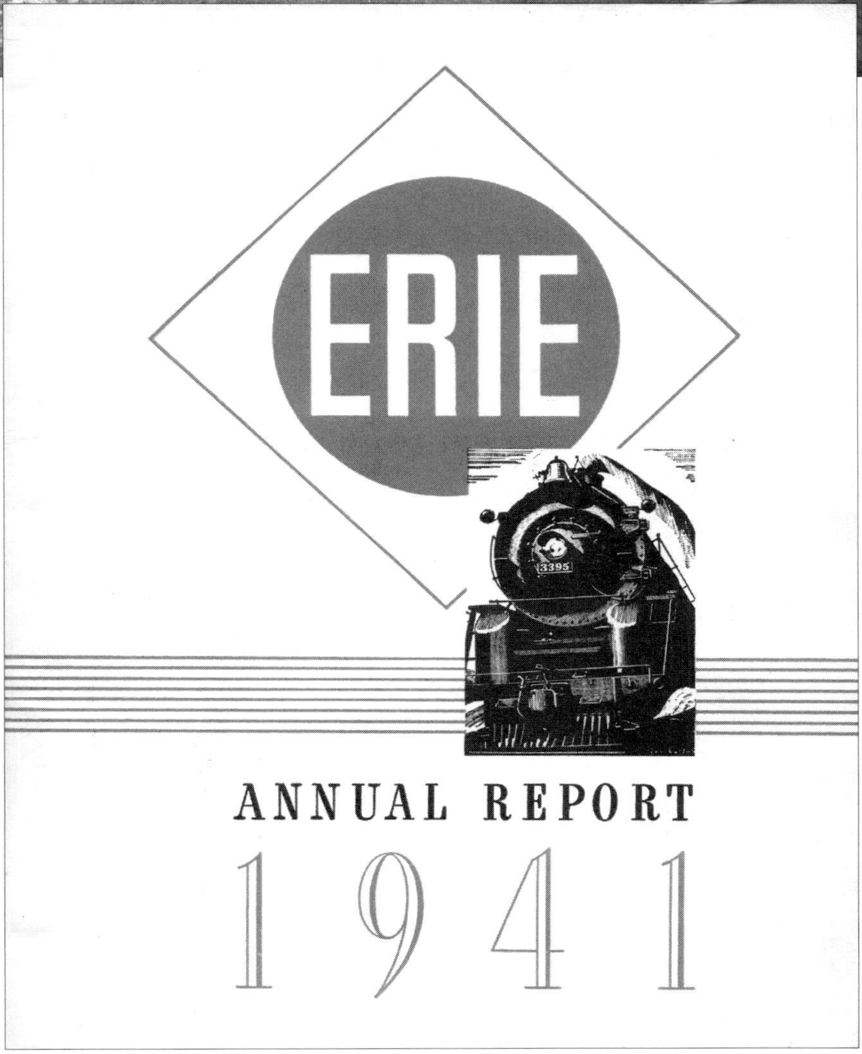

Erie was proud of its workhorse Berkshires, and used the face of No. 3395 at speed on the cover of its 1941 Annual Report. (TLC Collection)

The Erie's photographer captured this view of S-4 3399 on the turntable at Salamanca, N.Y. in 1947. This, the largest locomotive on the railroad, barely fit on the turntable. (Erie Railroad photo, Karen Parker collection)

S-4 No. 392 bangs across the diamonds at Lima, Ohio on July 10, 1933. (C.W. Jersstrom photo, Allen County Historical Society Collection)

C&O was one of the strongest if not the strongest proponent of the Superpower concept, and bought 132 locomotives of this type from Lima, more than any other railroad. This fleet consisted of 12 of the 4-8-4 wheel arrangement, 20 of the 2-8-4 type, 40 of the 2-10-4s, and 60 of the giant 2-6-6-6 type. C&O also bought 70 2-8-4s from Alco and 13 4-6-4s from Baldwin to round out its Super Power fleet. However, C&O will always be known for its Lima engines and as a great proponent and supporter of the concept as built by Lima.

C&O's first venture into the Super Power age came in 1930, when it received 40 truly giant 2-10-4s from Lima, given C&O class designation T-1. These locomotives were intended exclusively for service between Russell, Kentucky, and Toledo, Ohio, where they hauled 14,000-plus-ton coal trains for transfer to Great Lakes shipping. C&O had just completed its new line which connected its mainline along the Kentucky side of the Ohio River with the Hocking Valley Railway's terminal in Columbus. The HV had been operated as a subsidiary by C&O since 1910, and in 1930 it was merged, mainly to use its level mainline between Columbus and Toledo. The 2-10-4 kept its "Texas" type designated, assigned when Lima sold its first to the Texas & Pacific in 1925 (see page 29).

1930 C&O was part of the Van Sweringen group of railroads, controlled by O. P. and M. J. Van Sweringen, Cleveland brothers who controlled NKP, C&O, HV, Pere Marquette, Erie, and had interests in other lines. These railroads, though they were operated as completely separate businesses, cooperated in some ways. One of those was the creation of a joint committee called the Advisory Mechanical Committee (AMC), which operated out of Cleveland, and helped with design for rolling stock and locomotives on all these roads. One of AMC's aims was to develop the optimum designs for each road's particular needs as a whole and at the same time standardizing as much as possible to achieve some economies of scale as well as to ensure the best design's use on all the Van Sweringen railroads. They worked closely with the mechanical departments of each of the railroads, and the outcome indeed was, among other things, a series of highly successful Super Power steam locomotives. (See page 58 for a fuller explanation of the AMC)

The C&O 2-10-4 was the AMC's first step into the Super Power arena, and a highly successful one. The giant boiler and huge firebox allowed it to produce more than adequate steam for sustained high power and speed. However, speed was not an overriding consideration on the C&O's heavy coal trains, though the quicker they could be gotten over the road the better, given the high

In this Lima builder broadside of C&O 2-10-4 No. 3004 it is certainly easy to discern the size and compactness of this locomotive which just exudes power. Yet, for all its size it doesn't seem ugly or ponderous. (TLC Collection)

CHESAPEAKE & OHIO CLASS T-1 NO. 3000-3039 ORDER NO. 1122									
DELIVERED		3000-3014: SEPTEMBER, 1930; 3015-3028: OCTOBER, 1930; 3029-3039: NOVEMBER, 1930				CONSTRUCTION NUMBERS		7516-7555	
WHEEL ARRANGEMENT		DRIVING WHEEL DIAMETER	CYLINDERS		BOILER		FIREBOX		
2-10-4		69"	DIAMETER	STROKE	DIAMETER	PRESSURE	LENGTH	WIDTH	GRATE AREA
			29"	34"	99¾"	260 p.s.i.	162"	108¼"	121.7 SQ.FT.
WHEEL BASE			TRACTIVE POWER		FACTOR OF ADHESION		TUBES AND FLUES		
DRIVING	ENGINE	ENGINE AND TENDER	MAIN CYLINDERS WITH BOOSTER				NUMBER	DIAMETER	LENGTH
24' 4"	49' 3"	99' 5¾"	91,584 lbs. 106,584 lbs.		4.07		59 275	2¼" 3½"	21'
AVERAGE WEIGHT IN WORKING ORDER, POUNDS					HEATING SURFACES, SQUARE FEET				
ON DRIVERS	TRUCK	TRAILER		TOTAL ENGINE	TUBES AND FLUES	FIREBOX & COMB. CHAM.	SYPHONS	TOTAL	SUPERHEATER
		FRONT AXLE	REAR AXLE						
373,000	61,000	66,000	66,000	566,000	5,990	477	168	6,635	3,030
TENDER									
TYPE	FUEL	WATER	WEIGHT, FULLY LOADED						
12 WHEEL	30 TONS	23,500 GALS	415,000 LBS.						

A Lima official stands inside the T-1's huge firebox to demonstrate its size. Note the three thermic syphons. (Lima Photo, TLC Collection)

Another view inside the T-1 firebox illustrates the three thermic syphons, which increased the heating surface available to help burn the fuel. (Lima Photo, TLC Collection)

The T-1 backhead was cluttered with controls, gauges, and instruments, typical of that of a "modern" Super Power locomotive. Of course the fireman's side was mainly occupied with controls for the stoker. The face of the steam gauge is not visible because it was double faced and could be seen by fireman and engineer. It is in the center above the firebox door near where the "1122" order number sign has been placed. (Lima Photo, TLC Collection)

The T-1's spacious tender held 23,500 gallons and 30 tons of coal, so that it could easily travel over a subdivision usually without the necessity to take on coal and water between terminals. (Lima Photo, TLC Collection)

T-1 No. 3002 hauls a coal train headed for the Great Lakes in 1946. The photo was taken at Riverton, Kentucky, along C&O's Cincinnati Division just out of the large coal yard at Russell. A few miles farther along the train will divert across the Ohio River on a monumental bridge, and head almost straight north to C&O's Lakes coal terminal at Presque Isle, near Toledo. (C&O Ry. Photo, C&O Hist. Soc. Coll. (Image No. CSPR-1004)

In this iconic image a T-1 is seen with a southbound empty hopper drag just after crossing the massive Limeville, Ky. bridge over the Ohio River in June, 1948. The T-1s were built for coal service on this line between Russell, Ky. and Toledo, via Columbus, replacing simple articulated 2-8-8-2 locomotives that were only five years old. (Gene Huddleston photo, COHS Collection, Image No. COHS-1210)

level of traffic at the time. Coming in 1930 at the onset of the Depression, they were the last new locomotives that C&O would buy until it came back to Lima in 1935 for five high-powered 4-8-4 passenger locomotives to supplement and replace some of its old 4-8-2s and heavy Pacifics on the mountain grades in Virginia and West Virginia.

Delivered in December 1935 these 4-8-4s were given class J-3 on C&O and the type was named "Greenbrier" rather than the traditional "Northern," simply because C&O, with its long-time

CHESAPEAKE & OHIO CLASS J-3 NO. 600-604 ORDER NO. 1131									
DELIVERED	DECEMBER, 1935					CONSTRUCTION NUMBERS		7627-7631	
WHEEL ARRANGEMENT		DRIVING WHEEL DIAMETER	CYLINDERS		BOILER		FIREBOX		
			DIAMETER	STROKE	DIAMETER	PRESSURE	LENGTH	WIDTH	GRATE AREA
4-8-4		72"	27½"	30"	91 11/16"	250 p.s.i.	150 1/16"	96¼"	100.3 SQ.FT.
WHEEL BASE			TRACTIVE POWER		FACTOR OF ADHESION		TUBES AND FLUES		
DRIVING	ENGINE	ENGINE AND TENDER	MAIN CYLINDERS WITH BOOSTER				NUMBER	DIAMETER	LENGTH
19' 3"	46' 10½"	98' 5¾"	66,960 lbs. 81,035 lbs.		4.08		65 220	2¼" 3½"	21'
AVERAGE WEIGHT IN WORKING ORDER, POUNDS					HEATING SURFACES, SQUARE FEET				
		TRAILER		TOTAL ENGINE	TUBES AND FLUES	FIREBOX & COMB. CHAM.	SYPHONS	TOTAL	SUPERHEATER
ON DRIVERS	TRUCK	FRONT AXLE	REAR AXLE						
273,000	89,500	53,000	61,500	477,000	5,013	396	129	5,538	2,342
TENDER									
TYPE	FUEL	WATER	WEIGHT, FULLY LOADED						
12 WHEEL	25 TONS	22,000 GALS	381,700 LBS.						

headquarters in Richmond, and still anchored in the South, didn't like the "Northern" name and used something more suited. (The name applied to a river and county on C&O in West Virginia, and the C&O-owned Greenbrier resort hotel.) They were also given names of Virginia Governors, the first named locomotives on C&O since the late 1860s.

C&O didn't order any additional Lima locomotives until the eve of World War II, when management felt the need for a couple more of the 4-8-4s for passenger operations which were building up considerably from their Depression-era levels. Lima built two more 4-8-4s to essentially the same specifications as the first batch of 1935, and delivered them in January 1942, just in time to handle the heavy war-time traffic.

At the same time the AMC designed what

C&O J-3 4-8-4 Greenbrier type No. 600 was decked out for its builder's photo with the stylish C&O "donut" herald on the tender and the name "Th. Jefferson" on the sand dome. The J-3s were the first C&O locomotives to be named since the early days, and fit in with the image the line was fostering, featuring its Virginia colonial heritage. (Lima Photo, TLC Collection)

Here No. 600, Thomas Jefferson, leaves that great man's city of Charlottesville, Virginia, in 1937 westbound with a train heavy in head-end business. Note the star decorations on the polished cylinder heads and air-pump shields, another characteristic of C&O passenger locomotives of the 1930s. (TLC Collection)

J-3 No. 602 powers C&O Train No. 4 The Sportsman through the Virginia countryside near Charlottesville in 1936. The big 4-8-4s were used between Charlottesville, Va., and Hinton, W. Va., over the Blue Ridge and Alleghany grades. (H. K. Vollrath Collection)

In its last months of use, No. 602 is shorn of all its 1930s decorations, has had its headlight moved down to the pilot deck and a new oval number board in its place, and had its Walschaerts valve gear replaced by Baker. It is seen here powering No. 4 eastward from White Sulphur Springs, W. Va., with many of the new streamlined cars in consist. Within a few months of this 1951 photo, it would be sidetracked by new E8 diesels. (Gene Huddleston Photo, H. H. Harwood, Jr. Collection)

No. 601 is switching Pullman cars in the park track area of C&O's White Sulphur Springs station, front door for the fabulous Greenbrier resort hotel, which C&O purchased and operated after 1910. The photo was taken June 9, 1949. (Richard J. Cook Photo, TLC Collection)

Broadside of 605, the Thomas Nelson, Jr., looks very much like its predecessors 600-604 except the steam dome and sandbox have reversed positions atop the boiler. (Lima Photo, TLC Collection)

CHESAPEAKE & OHIO CLASS J-3 NO. 605-606 ORDER NO. 1156									
DELIVERED	JANUARY, 1942						CONSTRUCTION NUMBERS	7842-7843	
WHEEL ARRANGEMENT	DRIVING WHEEL DIAMETER		CYLINDERS		BOILER		FIREBOX		
4-8-4	72"		DIAMETER	STROKE	DIAMETER	PRESSURE	LENGTH	WIDTH	GRATE AREA
			27½"	30"	$91\frac{11}{16}$"	255 p.s.i.	$150\frac{1}{16}$"	96¼"	100.3 SQ.FT.
WHEEL BASE			TRACTIVE POWER		FACTOR OF ADHESION		TUBES AND FLUES		
DRIVING	ENGINE	ENGINE AND TENDER	MAIN CYLINDERS WITH BOOSTER				NUMBER	DIAMETER	LENGTH
19' 3"	46' 10½"	98' 5¾"	68,300 lbs. 82,700 lbs.		4.24		62 220	2¼" 3½"	21'
AVERAGE WEIGHT IN WORKING ORDER, POUNDS					HEATING SURFACES, SQUARE FEET				
ON DRIVERS	TRUCK	TRAILER		TOTAL ENGINE	TUBES AND FLUES	FIREBOX & COMB. CHAM.	SYPHONS	TOTAL	SUPERHEATER
		FRONT AXLE	REAR AXLE						
290,000	92,000	60,500	61,000	503,500	4,974	396	124	5,494	2,365
TENDER									
TYPE	FUEL	WATER	WEIGHT, FULLY LOADED						
12 WHEEL	25 TONS	22,000 GALS	388,020 LBS.						

The clean, elegant front of No. 602 looks out on the Charlottesville engine terminal as it pauses between runs in 1936. C&O later lowered the headlight to the pilot beam and centered the number plate on the smoke box door. (W. R. Osborne Photo, C&O Hist. Soc. Coll.)

By the time Nos. 605-606 arrived in early 1942, C&O's standard put the headlight on the pilot beam and the oval number plate on the smoke box. Shorn of all the 1930s decorations except the polished cylinder heads, the "war babies" had a different look. Note the sheet metal flag holders behind the Pyle National class lamps. Oval number plate was cast brass with polished number and red background. (Lima Photo, TLC Collection)

The large rectangular tender of Nos. 605-606 held 25 tons of coal and 22,000 gallons of water, which was enough to get it over the Blue Ridge between Charlottesville and Clifton Forge and from that point over Alleghany mountain to Hinton. The 4-8-4s were used exclusively between Charlottesville and Hinton, often changing at Clifton Forge, and sometimes only taking water. (Lima Photo, TLC Collection)

No. 606 is at Charlottesville in 1949, probably involved in consist adjustment, since at this point trains were divided or combined based on which line cars were headed. (M. D. McCarter Collection)

Opposite: Lima detail photo shows the cylinder and smoke box area of Thomas Nelson, Jr. (C&O No. 605). Note that six pipes lead from the sand box, enough to sand in front of all four axles, behind one, plus one for the booster. Note the multiple bearing crosshead and Baker Valve gear. (Lima Photo, TLC Collection)

The Sportsman, *Train No. 4/46 is eastbound near the summit of Blue Ridge at Afton, Virginia in July 1949 amid the mountain scenery that was the haunt of these mountain haulers. (J. I. Kelly Photo, C&O Hist. Soc. Coll., Image No. COHS-360)*

most would later call the ultimate Super Power locomotive for use on C&O's Alleghany grade between Hinton, West Virginia, and Clifton Forge, Virginia. This was the famous 2-6-6-6 Allegheny type. (Note that the locomotive type name is spelled with an "e", but the C&O's Subdivision, the county, and the town in this part of Virginia were spelled with an "a.")

The first of these giants arrived at Clifton Forge, Virginia, in December 1941 and were given class H-8 designation. More orders were completed during the war, and a final batch arrived in December 1948, rounding out a total of 60. In addition to handling heavy coal trains eastward over the Alleghany grade (with a second 2-6-6-6 pushing to the summit), they were eventually used to supplant the original C&O Super Power T-1 2-10-4s hauling coal through Ohio to the Lakes, and along the mainline on manifest freights. Many were equipped with steam and signal lines and helped out with passenger business during the war.

C&O's other Super Power type was the 2-8-4 which, of course, was the type used by Lima to introduce the concept back in 1925. Van Sweringen-controlled NKP received locomotives of this type in 1934; locomotives whose design was based on the design of the C&O T-1 but were built by Alco rather than Lima. Pere Marquette Railway of Michigan and Ontario also acquired

CHESAPEAKE & OHIO CLASS H-8 NO. 1600-1609 ORDER NO. 1154
CHESAPEAKE & OHIO CLASS H-8 NO. 1610-1619 ORDER NO. 1162
CHESAPEAKE & OHIO CLASS H-8 NO. 1620-1629 ORDER NO. 1182
CHESAPEAKE & OHIO CLASS H-8 NO. 1630-1644 ORDER NO. 1188

DELIVERED	1600-1605: DECEMBER, 1941; 1606-1609: JANUARY, 1942 1610-1616: SEPTEMBER, 1942; 1617-1619: OCTOBER, 1942 1620-1627: JULY, 1944; 1628-1629: AUGUST, 1944 1630-1631: OCTOBER, 1944; 1632-1637: NOVEMBER, 1944; 1638-1644: DECEMBER, 1944					CONSTRUCTION NUMBERS		1600-1609: 7820-7829 1610-1619: 7883-7892 1620-1629: 8613-8622 1630-1644: 8799-8813	
WHEEL ARRANGEMENT		DRIVING WHEEL DIAMETER	CYLINDERS		BOILER		FIREBOX		
			DIAMETER	STROKE	DIAMETER	PRESSURE	LENGTH	WIDTH	GRATE AREA
2-6-6-6		67"	22½"	33"	109"	260 p.s.i.	180"	108$^{1}/_{8}$"	135.2 SQ.FT.
WHEEL BASE			TRACTIVE POWER		FACTOR OF ADHESION		TUBES AND FLUES		
DRIVING	ENGINE	ENGINE AND TENDER	MAIN CYLINDERS				NUMBER	DIAMETER	LENGTH
34' 8"	62' 6"	112' 11"	110,200 lbs.		4.61		48 278	2¼" 3½"	23'
AVERAGE WEIGHT IN WORKING ORDER, POUNDS					HEATING SURFACES, SQUARE FEET				
ON DRIVERS	TRUCK	TRAILER		TOTAL ENGINE	TUBES AND FLUES	FIREBOX & COMB. CHAM.	SYPHONS	TOTAL	SUPERHEATER
507,900	71,300	192,100		771,300	6,478	600	162	7,240	3,186
TENDER									
TYPE	FUEL	WATER	WEIGHT, FULLY LOADED						
14 WHEEL	25 TONS	25,000 GALS	437,600 LBS.						

NOTE: THE WEIGHTS ON THESE LOCOMOTIVES WERE INITIALLY UNDER-REPORTED AT 724,500 lbs., AND THOSE WEIGHTS WERE WIDELY PUBLISHED, EVEN BY LIMA. THE VALUES SHOW IN THIS TABLE ARE CORRECT, BASED ON THE ORIGINAL LIMA SCALE REPORTS. SEE *THE ALLEGHENY, LIMA'S FINEST* BY EUGENE L. HUDDLESTON AND THOMAS W. DIXON, JR. FOR MORE DETAILS.

CHESAPEAKE & OHIO CLASS H-8 NO. 1645-1659 ORDER NO. 1205

DELIVERED	1645-1649: OCTOBER, 1948; 1650-1654: NOVEMBER, 1948; 1655-1659: DECEMBER, 1948					CONSTRUCTION NUMBERS		9309-9323	
WHEEL ARRANGEMENT		DRIVING WHEEL DIAMETER	CYLINDERS		BOILER		FIREBOX		
			DIAMETER	STROKE	DIAMETER	PRESSURE	LENGTH	WIDTH	GRATE AREA
2-6-6-6		67"	22½"	33"	109"	260 p.s.i.	180"	108$^{1}/_{8}$"	135.3 SQ.FT.
WHEEL BASE			TRACTIVE POWER		FACTOR OF ADHESION		TUBES AND FLUES		
DRIVING	ENGINE	ENGINE AND TENDER	MAIN CYLINDERS				NUMBER	DIAMETER	LENGTH
34' 8"	62' 6"	112' 11"	110,200 lbs.		4.57		48 278	2¼" 3½"	23'
AVERAGE WEIGHT IN WORKING ORDER, POUNDS					HEATING SURFACES, SQUARE FEET				
ON DRIVERS	TRUCK	TRAILER		TOTAL ENGINE	TUBES AND FLUES	FIREBOX & COMB. CHAM.	SYPHONS	TOTAL	SUPERHEATER
504,010	65,570	182,250		751,830	6,032	600	162	6,795	2,922
TENDER									
TYPE	FUEL	WATER	WEIGHT, FULLY LOADED						
14 WHEEL	25 TONS	25,000 GALS	431,710 LBS.						

From the second order of H-8 2-6-6-6s, Lima builder broadside No. 1610 well shows its massive firebox and the six-wheel truck needed to support it, as well as the huge tender with both six- and eight-wheel trucks. So pleased with the T-1 2-10-4s, C&O wanted to expand it to a 2-12-4, but decided to divide the drivers into two engines both to provide additional flexibility in operation, but also to increase the power. (Lima Photo, TLC Collection)

A left side portrait of C&O H-8 No. 1633 ready for shipment from Lima. Note the jacketing over the firebox, which covered insulation and thus prevented additional heat loss. (Lima Photo, TLC Collection)

Perhaps no other angle could portray the size, complexity, and powerful appearance of a C&O H-8. Here No. 1603, one of the first out of the Lima erecting shop in late 1941 shows off the large, high pilot deck that allowed easy access to the front-mounted air pumps, after-cooler grill, and smoke box door. Giant pipes conducted high pressure steam. The monstrous sand domes supplied traction as the giants lumbered up steep grades with heavy coal trains or speeded fast manifests. (Lima Photo, TLC Collection)

Opposite Center: In the late 1940s, when C&O had acquired an ever larger fleet of H-8 2-6-6-6s, they began to supplement the 1930-era T-1 2-10-4s on the coal trains through Ohio to the Great Lakes. Here an H-8 takes empties back toward to coal fields in a broadside action photo near Parsons yard in Columbus, in 1950. (W. G. Francher photo, C&O Hist. Soc. Coll.).

Opposite Bottom: This 1942 C&O publicity photo lined up three of the new giant H-8 2-6-6-6s at their home terminal of Clifton Forge, Va. It was used in many C&O advertisements in the era. (C&O Ry. Photo, C&O Hist. Soc. Coll., Image No, CSPR-57.038)

The cluttered front-end of an H-8 was quite utilitarian, but not very pleasing aesthetically. (Lima Photo, TLC Collection)

H-8s were also used to power coal trains along C&O's New River Subdivision mainline west of Hinton, as is the case with No. 1642 at Cotton Hill, W. Va., in this photo taken about 1949. In 1953 this locomotive exploded at Hinton, killing its crew in a spectacular accident. (B. F. Cutler photo, TLC Collection)

As soon as C&O received its first H-8s, it took a series of publicity photos, including this one, showing one of the giants on a big coal train about to reach the top of Alleghany grade, at Tuckahoe, W. Va., in January 1942. C&O Ry. Photo, TLC Collection)

This sequence of photos shows H-8s in their most common duty, pulling heavy coal trains eastward over Alleghany Mountain. Caught in action on Thanksgiving Day in 1950 at White Sulphur Springs, W. Va., No. 1616 is on the head-end, while 1630 is pushing hard from the rear. When the train reached the summit, the pusher would cut off and return light to Hinton. (Gene Huddleston Photos, C&O Hist. Soc. Collection)

this wheel arrangement in 1937 (See page 98), and another Van Sweringen road, the Erie, had received 2-8-4s of a related but earlier design in 1927 (see page 61).

Interestingly enough, C&O received only 20 of its eventual fleet of 90 2-8-4s from Lima (and these came in a batch of 10 in 1945 and a final 10 in 1947). Classed K-4, they were named "Kanawha Type" on C&O, again using a West Virginia river as the name, since they would spend much of their lives along its banks. The other 70 C&O Kanawhas, including the first group) came from Alco.

At the same time that C&O was getting its 2-8-4s, another AMC road, the Nickel Plate, received its first Lima 2-8-4s (see page 89), of a very similar design and look, rightly so because though the Van Sweringen empire had broken up by then, PM and NKP were still controlled by C&O and the AMC was still in operation for design work. Erie had gone its own way.

When almost all other railroads had opted for dieselization in one form or other following the war, C&O stuck to steam, and did so with considerable publicity, as did its neighbors Norfolk & Western, and Virginian, believing that they had to support their major business, hauling coal. Therefore, when post-war motive power orders were planned, steam was at the forefront. At this time C&O was experimenting with a steam-turbine-electric that it hoped would preserve the "coal fired" locomotive, though not of the reciprocating type. Ultimately this failed.

In 1947 C&O ordered a large number of reciprocating steam of tried and true designs, which was delivered in 1947-49. This included final batches of fifteen 2-6-6-6s, five 4-8-4s, and ten 2-8-4s from Lima. Although these were among the last Super Power locomotives built by Lima (or anyone else), they weren't quite the last, that designation being held by the final group of Lima NKP 2-8-4s in mid-1949. Louisville & Nashville also received its last steam locomotives in the form of its M-1 class Lima-built 2-8-4s in mid-1949.

The K-4 class 2-8-4s from Lima looks almost exactly like those of the class built by Alco, and had the typical C&O face of the era: high bell between two lighted number boards, centered number plate, low headlight on the pilot beam, above shielded pumps and aftercoolers. Oval number plate was painted black with yellow numerals. The smoke box front was painted graphite. In 1942 AMC decreed a standard Pyle National lighted number board, and the K-4s came with this installed new. (Lima Photo, TLC Collection)

Although C&O received 90 2-8-4 types between 1943 and 1948, Lima built only 20 of them, in 1945 and 1947. Here No. 2744 poses for its builder broadside. A comparison of this photo with other builder views of the C&O's T-1, J-3, and even H-8s, shows that there were definite similarities. (Lima photo, TLC Collection).

CHESAPEAKE & OHIO CLASS K-4 NO. 2740-2749 ORDER NO. 1192 CHESAPEAKE & OHIO CLASS K-4 NO. 2750-2759 ORDER NO. 1198									
DELIVERED	2740: SEPTEMBER, 1945; 2741-2744: OCTOBER, 1945; 2745-2746: NOVEMBER, 1945; 2747-2749: DECEMBER, 1945 2750-2753: JANUARY, 1947; 2754-2758: FEBRUARY, 1947; 2759: MARCH, 1947					CONSTRUCTION NUMBERS		2740-2749: 9047-9056 2750-2759: 9257-9266	
WHEEL ARRANGEMENT	DRIVING WHEEL DIAMETER		CYLINDERS		BOILER		FIREBOX		
			DIAMETER	STROKE	DIAMETER	PRESSURE	LENGTH	WIDTH	GRATE AREA
2-8-4	69"		26"	34"	87 15/16"	245 p.s.i.	135 1/16"	96 1/4"	90.3 SQ.FT.
WHEEL BASE			TRACTIVE POWER		FACTOR OF ADHESION		TUBES AND FLUES		
DRIVING	ENGINE	ENGINE AND TENDER	MAIN CYLINDERS WITH BOOSTER				NUMBER	DIAMETER	LENGTH
18' 3"	42' 0"	93' 2"	69,350 lbs. 83,350 lbs.		4.22 (a) 4.23 (b)		73 202	2 1/4" 3 1/2"	19'
AVERAGE WEIGHT IN WORKING ORDER, POUNDS					HEATING SURFACES, SQUARE FEET				
		TRAILER		TOTAL ENGINE	TUBES AND FLUES	FIREBOX & COMB. CHAM.	SYPHONS	TOTAL	SUPERHEATER
ON DRIVERS	TRUCK	FRONT AXLE	REAR AXLE						
292,600 (a) 293,100 (b)	47,900 48,500	61,300 61,100	67,100 66,980	468,900 469,680	4,308	344 343	122 63 (circulators)	4,774 4714	1,932
TENDER									
TYPE	FUEL	WATER	WEIGHT, 2/3 LOADED						
12 WHEEL	30 TONS	21,000 GALS	315,090 LBS.						

Note: No. 2750-2759 were equipped with four circulators in the fire box rather than the Thermic Syphons used in 2740-2749. This had a minor effect on the weights and heating surfaces of this group of locomotives, as shown in the second lines, labeled "(b)", in the weight and heating surface boxes in the table.

C&O certainly was the biggest buyer and most vigorous supporter of Lima and its modern steam. The post-WWII view that diesels had not yet killed steam and there was room left for the old technology was shared by the managements of both Lima and C&O--at least until there was no choice.

C&O began buying diesels for its old mainlines in 1949 (it had merged the Pere Marquette in 1947, and that line was already dieselizing). By 1954 about 80% of all C&O operations were diesel, and the last steam operated in the fall of 1956. Many of the later Lima Super Power locomotives had only a very short operating life before being sidelined by diesels.

Visible in this close-up photo of the back end of K-4 No. 2754 are the turret in front of the cab, the top of the blow-down muffler, and the shield around the pop valves, all on top of the boiler. Below the cab behind the trailing truck are the rear frame support resting on the back of the truck, the booster engine and its piping, and the Nathan non-lifting injector, along with its attached cold water feed lines from the tender. Careful observation will also reveal the sand pipe for the booster, just ahead of the rear wheel on the truck. (Lima photo, TLC Collection)

Lima-built K-4 No. 2747 was only about a year old when this photo was taken in September 1946 as it wheeled a fast freight eastward across the Big Sandy River bridge between Kentucky and West Virginia en route from Chicago to Newport News and Washington. The K-4s were used in all types of work: coal trains, fast freights locals, branch runs, and even passenger trains. (C&O Ry. Photo, C&O Hist. Soc. Coll., Image No. 57.174)

Hauling a fast freight train up the Big Sandy Branch in eastern Kentucky, usually the haunt of coal trains, No. 2743 is headed for a connection with the Clinchfield Railroad at Elkhorn City, Ky., in about 1948 to exchange fast freight for the south. (C&O Ry. Photo, C&O Hist. Soc. Coll. , Image No. CSPR-3350)

A good overhead view of Lima K-4 No. 2751 entering the yard at Handley, West Virginia, in 1953 with train of loads from the coal fields, and about half of its fuel load consumed. (Joe Collias Photo)

CHESAPEAKE & OHIO CLASS J-3A NO. 610-614 ORDER NO. 1201									
DELIVERED		JUNE, 1948				CONSTRUCTION NUMBERS		9302-9306	
WHEEL ARRANGEMENT		DRIVING WHEEL DIAMETER	CYLINDERS		BOILER		FIREBOX		
4-8-4		72"	DIAMETER	STROKE	DIAMETER	PRESSURE	LENGTH	WIDTH	GRATE AREA
			27½"	30"	$91^{11}/_{16}$"	255 p.s.i.	$150^{1}/_{16}$"	96¼"	100.3 SQ.FT.
WHEEL BASE			TRACTIVE POWER		FACTOR OF ADHESION		TUBES AND FLUES		
DRIVING	ENGINE	ENGINE AND TENDER	MAIN CYLINDERS WITH BOOSTER				NUMBER	DIAMETER	LENGTH
19' 3"	47' 1"	98' 7¾"	66,450 lbs. 78,850 lbs.		4.29		62 220	2¼" 3½"	21'
AVERAGE WEIGHT IN WORKING ORDER, POUNDS					HEATING SURFACES, SQUARE FEET				
ON DRIVERS	TRUCK	TRAILER		TOTAL ENGINE	TUBES AND FLUES	FIREBOX & COMB. CHAM.	CIRCULATORS	TOTAL	SUPERHEATER
		FRONT AXLE	REAR AXLE						
290,000	81,600	55,600	59,800	482,200	4,339	417	65	4,821	2,058
TENDER									
TYPE	FUEL	WATER	WEIGHT, FULLY LOADED						
12 WHEEL	25 TONS	21,500 GALS	386,130 LBS.						

The typical Lima right broadside builder photo shows how similar in appearance the J-3a is with other C&O Super Power locomotives. One difference from the J-3s of 1935-1942 is that the steam dome and sandbox are placed in the same casing. The large cast steel pilot is a carry-over from when this locomotive was initially designed with a streamlined cowl. The streamlining was eliminated before construction. (Lima Photo, TLC Collection)

This excellent ¾ view of J-3a No. 610 shows the solid pilot well. See also are the Baker valve gear, tandem side rods, and box pok drivers. The bell was air-actuated and non-swinging. The protrusion right behind the stack is the whistle. Lima used this particular photo for many of its late steam-era advertisements, including an air-brushed version that added poppet valves and Belpre boiler! (Lima Photo, TLC Collection)

Above Left: J-3a tender under construction. This photo from inside the coal bunker shows the screw mechanism of the stoker. (Lima Photo, TLC Collection)

Above Right: The last J-3a, No. 614, has Train No. 46, the Virginia section of The Sportsman in tow at Marshall Street, just before arriving at Richmond's Main Street Station May 27, 1950. (D. Wallace Johnson Photo)

A nice left side ¾ view of No. 610 shows the arrangement of the fireman's side in this view taken at Richmond June 26, 1952, as it was serving its last months on passenger trains before being sidetracked by diesels after only just over three years' service. These locomotives had Timken roller bearing siderods. (A. A. Thieme Photo, TLC Collection)

After the J-3a class 4-8-4s were replaced with diesels on passenger trains, they were put to work on freights, but then were bumped by diesels again and they were stored serviceable. Then in 1955-56, when an unexpected increase in coal business overtaxed available diesels, some were called back to service. Here 610 is handling an empty coal train leaving Russell, Kentucky, in June 1955. (Gene Huddleston photo, C&O Hist. Soc. Coll., Image No. COHS-2023)

Opposite Center: At the very end of its career, 613 was given a set of experimental smoke deflectors, used on only one other C&O locomotive. This photo shows it in service on Train No. 41, the Virginia section of the westbound George Washington, at Williamsburg, with new lightweight streamlined cars behind the express car, in 1951. E-8s were already bumping the big 4-8-4s from their mountain duties on the Washington-Cincinnati main stem, and 613 is was now hauling the short (6 car) Virginia sections of the trains between Charlottesville and Newport News, until enough diesels arrived to replace it in this work as well. (W. B. Gwaltney Photo)

J-3a 614 was retained by C&O after its retirement, and eventually was put on display at the B&O Railroad Museum. In 1979 it was sold to Ross Rowland, who refurbished it and ran it for Chessie System as "Chessie Safety Express." Then, in the winter of 1984-85 Rowland and CSX placed it in regular coal train operations Huntington-Hinton for a month to test the viability of returning to coal-fueled locomotives in Rowland's "ACE-3000" project. Here "614-T" (T for test) has a train of empty hoppers near the station at Charleston, W.Va., on January 24, 1985. No. 614 is today stored and capable of being rebuilt for service, one of Lima's last Super Power locomotives. (Jay Potter Photo)

722
722
722

Nickel Plate Road (New York, Chicago & St. Louis)

One of the roads that is most especially remembered for its modern Lima-built Superpower locomotives is the Nickel Plate Road (NKP), which rostered only one Super Power wheel arrangement, the 2-8-4 Berkshire Type.

NKP was also one of the Van Sweringen Roads. In fact, it was the first railroad that Cleveland real estate developers O. P. and M. J. Van Sweringen bought, in 1916. From it they expanded their empire so that by the beginning of the Depression they controlled, though a maze of holding companies, the NKP, C&O, Pere Marquette, Erie, and had major holdings in other railroads.

When NKP came to the Vans it was not in very good condition, having existed most of its life as a poor stepchild of the New York Central, but under the Van Sweringens, and most especially with the guidance of John J. Bernet, who at one time or another and sometimes at the same time was president of it and the other Van Sweringen roads. The brothers were the financial wizards that made the empire (and lost it during the Depression), but it was Bernet (coming from NYC to be NKP president in 1916) that they used as their main railroad man.

With a lot of its business overhead or "bridge" traffic, and in a very competitive geographical environment, NKP needed to do better than some of its nearby competitors to attract business. It would eventually settle on the winning formula of very speedy and high quality service.

In 1927 the Erie was in the process of buying "Super Power" 2-8-4s. Forty-Five of these came from Lima (see page 59), while virtual duplicates arrived from Alco (25), and Baldwin (35). They allowed obsolete engines to be retired. increased train speed, and moved more gross tons by very considerable margins.

In 1929 the Advisory Mechanical Committee was created, to oversee and coordinate the mechanical design efforts of the Van Sweringen railroads. Using the best talent from the constituent lines, with a heavy influence from Erie, the committee designed all the Super Power locomotive purchased over the next two decades by NKP, Erie, C&O, and Pere Marquette. (See page 57)

It used the Erie 2-8-4's that were recognized as so successful, to develop the giant C&O T-1 2-10-4 of 1930 (see page 67), by, as some historians have said, "slide-ruling" up its dimensions.

Opposite: No. 722 is handling a long troop train westbound near Brewster, Ohio, in October 1945 as troops return from overseas for demobilization. The Berks were easily able to handle large troop trains at speed, and many were equipped with steam and communication lines. (William Rittasse Photo, Jay Williams Collection)

NKP bought four 4-6-4 Pacifics from Lima in 1929, which, of course, qualify as Super Power because of their four-wheel trailing truck if not their total furnace capacity. These locomotives were stars with NKP passenger trains up to the end of steam. AMC likely didn't have any great influence on their design because they were ordered at about the same time that the AMC was being organized.

After the C&O got its 2-10-4s the Depression intervened and it was not until 1934 that NKP was allowed to order new locomotives. When finally allowed to get new power, it opted for 2-8-4s. Using the C&O T-1 as a base, the dimensions were down-sized to fit the new design. The NKP design had about 30% less weight and tractive power as the C&O locomotives, and didn't have a booster. The resulting S-class NKP Berkshires looked very much like a smaller version of C&O T-1s.

Once the new design had been settled, an order for 15 locomotives was placed with Alco. Although Lima might have been the first choice, a federal loan as part of Depression-era programs, required that the order be competitively bid, and Alco won, much to Lima's chagrin as its plant had been closed since the C&O T-1s had been completed in 1930.

Alco's Schenectady Works built the 2-8-4s, which NKP classed "S," delivering them to NKP in November 1934. These locomotives became a mainstay of NKP's high-class fast freight service west of Cleveland. At 64,100 pounds of tractive effort and an ample firebox of 135x96 inches, with 90.3 square feet of grates, evaporative surface of 4,818, and 1,992 square feet of superheater, these locomotives could handle about anything that NKP wanted, and did it very well. If fact, they were so well liked that NKP ordered no other wheel arrangement for its mainline freight service and virtually duplicated these dimensions up the end of steam. In this case the VERY end of steam, as NKP Berkshire No. 779 was the last Super Power locomotive built by Lima or anyone, for that matter.

The face of the S class looked very much like that of the C&O T-1s with a centered headlight with number plate suspended, bell at the top of the firebox, and shielded pumps on the pilot beam. With 69-inch drivers, these locomotives could take full advantage of their ability to create horsepower at speed.

Their tenders were equipped with six-wheel trucks and held 22 tons and 22,000 gallons.

Top to Bottom: Builders photos of the S-1, S-2, and S-3 class Berkshires. (Lima Photos, Allen County Hist. Soc. Coll.)

They were able to increase speed for manifest freights and generally helped to increase NKP's ability to move its freight. The country was still in the Depression at this time, so NKP wasn't able to add any additional 2-8-4s to its roster until the coming of World War II, but the 15 Alco Super Power locomotives (following all the precepts laid down by Lima over the preceding decade) did a superb job.

It was not until the advent of World War II that NKP was finally able to expand its fleet of 2-8-4s, and this time it bought all its locomotives from Lima. Ordered in early 1942, Lima wasn't able to complete them until the spring of 1943 because of a backlog of work not only of locomotives but of other war-related production as well. Finally delivered in June and July 1943, the 15 new Berkshires went to work handling the massive war-time demand that had been placed on all American railroads. They were given S-1 class designation by NKP.

The S-1s were essentially duplicates of the S class that had been built by Alco, first because of the success of this type and because the AMC was still controlling orders for NKP locomotives. The Van Sweringen empire had broken up during the Depression, but C&O still maintained control of Pere Marquette and NKP, and continued the AMC for its joint mechanical work. The S-1s were a little heavier than the original S class, and looked identical.

Quickly realizing that the war effort required even more new motive power, the AMC and NKP ordered another 10 Berkshires with S-1 classification, which Lima delivered March-May 1943. Yet another order for 2-8-4s was given Lima, and the 15 new S-2 class Berks were delivered January-March 1944, just as the war traffic was peaking, and another 15 came late that year. The S-2s were heavier yet and were also equipped with roller bearings on the drivers and engine truck. They also had a factor of adhesion of 4.12. Their overall appearance, however, was not different from the S and S-1 classes.

In 1943 the NKP strengthened certain bridges which allowed Berkshires to operate east of Cleveland through to Buffalo for the first time, supplanting old 2-8-2s which had handled the traffic in that region. They were also moved into other areas when bridge restrictions were corrected.

Several of the S-1 and S-2 classes were equipped with steam and communication lines for use as needed in passenger service, especially for troop trains. In the 1950s some of these were used in some excursion trains during the waning days of steam.

After the end of the war, almost all railroads began a headlong dash into dieselization. Not so with NKP.

Although diesels were tested, NKP remained committed to steam, though perhaps not as vociferously as C&O and N&W.

In the summer of 1948 NKP ordered what would be its final batch of 2-8-4s from Lima, which arrived between March and May 1949. No. 779 of this group was the very last Super Power locomotive to leave the Lima plant. Indeed, in 1947 Lima had merged with the General Machinery Company of Hamilton, Ohio, to become Lima-Hamilton, and would eventually merge with the ancient Baldwin Locomotive Works, to become Baldwin-Lima-Hamilton. It attempted diesel production at the Lima plant, but was never successful. However, it left the steam locomotive field on the highest of notes, not only with the final order of the superb NKP 2-8-4s, but also with great Super Power locomotives of 2-8-4, 4-8-4, and 2-6-6-6 designs for C&O in 1948.

The NKP S-3 class, as this final order was designated, had a considerable additional weight, a factor of adhesion of 4.17 and according to Kevin Holland writing in the standard reference for these locomotives (*Nickel Plate Berkshires*, published by TLC Publishing, 1998) says that NKP and Lima decided on no less than 97 improvements over the war-time locomotives, but that some compromises were necessary because suppliers of parts and devices were going out of business or changing their product lines because all other commercial builders were converting to strictly diesel production.

It should be noted also that by this time the AMC of C&O, NKP and PM had been broken up and that C&O merged PM into its structure in 1947. In the same year C&O divested itself of its NKP control.

No. 779, the last of Lima, was sent by NKP to the Chicago Railroad Fair in 1949 and represented the railroad there for several months in company with many flashy diesels and steam turbines.

The NKP Berkshires continued their fast freight duties, but the inevitability of diesels was soon enough recognized, and the last of the line were used in their accustomed service as diesels arrived to supplant them gradually over many parts of the system. By late 1958 the last steam had operated in revenue service and after a period of being stored in case of need the Berkshires were scrapped. No. 755 was donated to Conneaut, Ohio, for display, and No. 779 went the Allen County Historical Society in Lima, Ohio, fittingly. No. 757 went to the Pennsylvania Railroad Museum in Strasburg, while No. 763 was sent to Roanoke, Virginia, for display in the Virginia Transportation Museum (it was removed in 2009 and sent to to a private owner in Ohio). No. 759 went to Nelson Blount for his Steamtown museum, was leased to Ross Rowland's High Iron Company, and powered the special *Golden Spike Centennial* train in 1969. It is now on display at Steamtown National Park in Scranton, Pennsylvania. No. 765 is currently in possession of the Fort Wayne Railroad Historical Society which has used it on many excursion trains over the years.

The last order of 10 NKP 2-8-4s was classed S-3, and No, 779 was the last, making it the last Super Power locomotive and the last of Lima, shown here at Cleveland shiny and polished en route to the Chicago Railroad Fair as part of NKP's exhibit. What a classic photo with the fast freight stretched out behind. (J. D. Burger Photo, Jay Williams Collection)

NICKEL PLATE ROAD CLASS S-1 NO. 715-729 ORDER NO. 1160
NICKEL PLATE ROAD CLASS S-1 NO. 730-739 ORDER NO. 1166

DELIVERED		CONSTRUCTION NUMBERS	
	715-722: JUNE, 1942; 723-739: JULY, 1942 730-734: MARCH, 1943; 735-736: APRIL, 1943; 737-739 MAY, 1943		715-729: 7860-7874 730-739: 8003-8012

WHEEL ARRANGEMENT	DRIVING WHEEL DIAMETER	CYLINDERS		BOILER		FIREBOX		
		DIAMETER	STROKE	DIAMETER	PRESSURE	LENGTH	WIDTH	GRATE AREA
2-8-4	69"	25"	34"	87 15/16"	245 p.s.i.	135 1/16"	96¼"	90.3 SQ.FT.

WHEEL BASE			TRACTIVE POWER	FACTOR OF ADHESION		TUBES AND FLUES		
DRIVING	ENGINE	ENGINE AND TENDER	MAIN CYLINDERS			NUMBER	DIAMETER	LENGTH
18' 3"	42' 0"	87' 8¾"	64,100 lbs.	4.02		73 202	2¼" 3½"	19'

AVERAGE WEIGHT IN WORKING ORDER, POUNDS					HEATING SURFACES, SQUARE FEET				
ON DRIVERS	TRUCK	TRAILER FRONT AXLE	TRAILER REAR AXLE	TOTAL ENGINE	TUBES AND FLUES	FIREBOX & COMB. CHAM.	ARCH TUBES & SYPHONS	TOTAL	SUPERHEATER
258,000	53,500	50,500	59,000	421,000	4,311	344	117	4,772	1,932

TENDER			
TYPE	FUEL	WATER	WEIGHT, 2/3 LOAD
12 WHEEL	22 TONS	22,000 GALS	283,400 LBS.

NICKEL PLATE ROAD CLASS S-2 NO. 740-754 ORDER NO. 1179
NICKEL PLATE ROAD CLASS S-2 NO. 755-769 ORDER NO. 1184

DELIVERED		CONSTRUCTION NUMBERS	
	740-745: JANUARY, 1944; 746-751: FEBRUARY, 1944; 752-754: MARCH, 1944 755-762: AUGUST, 1944; 763-769: SEPTEMBER, 1944		740-754: 8414-8428 755-769: 8663-8677

WHEEL ARRANGEMENT	DRIVING WHEEL DIAMETER	CYLINDERS		BOILER		FIREBOX		
		DIAMETER	STROKE	DIAMETER	PRESSURE	LENGTH	WIDTH	GRATE AREA
2-8-4	69"	25"	34"	87 15/16"	245 p.s.i.	135 1/16"	96¼"	90.3 SQ.FT.

WHEEL BASE			TRACTIVE POWER	FACTOR OF ADHESION		TUBES AND FLUES		
DRIVING	ENGINE	ENGINE AND TENDER	MAIN CYLINDERS			NUMBER	DIAMETER	LENGTH
18' 3"	40' 0"	87' 8¾"	64,100 lbs.	*4.12*		73 202	2¼" 3½"	19'

AVERAGE WEIGHT IN WORKING ORDER, POUNDS					HEATING SURFACES, SQUARE FEET				
ON DRIVERS	TRUCK	TRAILER FRONT AXLE	TRAILER REAR AXLE	TOTAL ENGINE	TUBES AND FLUES	FIREBOX & COMB. CHAM.	ARCH TUBES & SYPHONS	TOTAL	SUPERHEATER
264,300	*54,000*	*61,300*	*61,200*	*440,800*	4,311	344	117	4,772	1,932

TENDER			
TYPE	FUEL	WATER	WEIGHT, FULLY LOADED
12 WHEEL	22 TONS	22,000 GALS	285,270 LBS.

Right side view of S-1 No. 739 taken at Madison, Illinois, in about 1948 shows a very dirty locomotive, its drivers and trailer white with crushed sand after some very hard work. (Jay Williams Collection)

NICKEL PLATE ROAD CLASS S-3 NO. 770-779 ORDER NO. 1209		
DELIVERED	770-773: MARCH, 1949; 774: APRIL, 1949; 775-779: MAY, 1949	CONSTRUCTION NUMBERS 9371-9380

WHEEL ARRANGEMENT	DRIVING WHEEL DIAMETER	CYLINDERS		BOILER		FIREBOX		
		DIAMETER	STROKE	DIAMETER	PRESSURE	LENGTH	WIDTH	GRATE AREA
2-8-4	69"	25"	34"	87 $^{15}/_{16}$"	245 p.s.i.	135 $^{1}/_{16}$"	96¼"	90.3 SQ.FT.

WHEEL BASE			TRACTIVE POWER	FACTOR OF ADHESION		TUBES AND FLUES		
DRIVING	ENGINE	ENGINE AND TENDER	MAIN CYLINDERS			NUMBER	DIAMETER	LENGTH
18' 3"	40' 0"	87' 8¾"	64,100 lbs.	4.15		73 202	2¼" 3½"	19'

AVERAGE WEIGHT IN WORKING ORDER, POUNDS					HEATING SURFACES, SQUARE FEET				
ON DRIVERS	TRUCK	TRAILER		TOTAL ENGINE	TUBES AND FLUES	FIREBOX & COMB. CHAM.	ARCH TUBES & SYPHONS	TOTAL	SUPERHEATER
		FRONT AXLE	REAR AXLE						
266,030	55,040	61,970	61,250	444,290	4,311	344	117	4,772	1,932

TENDER			
TYPE	FUEL	WATER	WEIGHT, $^{2}/_{3}$ LOAD
12 WHEEL	22 TONS	22,000 GALS	288,840 LBS.

Probably the quintessential NKP Berkshire photo, No. 738 is wheeling the "Flying Saucer" fast freight over a trestle at Westfield, New York with 60 cars of fast freight at 2:30 pm Oct. 16, 1953. (R. R. Malinowski Photo, Jay Williams Collection)

Left side view of S-1 No. 739 shows appliances on the fireman's side of the of Berkshire as it rests from its work at NKP's Lima terminal in 1948. From this angle the air pump is visible behind its pilot deck shielding. (Jay Williams Collection)

S-1 No. 727 rides the turntable at Bellevue, Ohio, in May 1958 during the last days of steam. This particular locomotive was taken out of service on June 23, 1958, just a month or so later. (Jay Williams Collection)

This masterful at-speed photo shows the drivers and rods of S-2 No. 743 rolling a fast freight near Erie, Pennsylvania, in the summer of 1956. It was late in the steam era, but the good NKP Berkshires were still on the "fast freight" job. (Robert O. Hale, Jay Williams Collection)

S-2 No. 743 is only three months old when this photo was made as it powered a westbound freight at Bay Village, Ohio, on May 27, 1944 at the height of World War II traffic. (Duane Bearse Photo, Jay Williams Collection)

NKP fast freight No. 98 with Piggyback trailers right behind S-3 No. 772 on the high bridge over Conneaut Creek near Conneaut, Ohio, with 85 cars of 76 loads and 9 empties aggregating 4,235 tons, at 1:15 pm Oct. 9, 1957. The train was en route from Chicago to Buffalo. (R. R. Malinoski photo, Jay Williams Collection)

A night photo accentuates the latent power of S-2 No. 744 at the Bellevue engine terminal, July 18, 1957. Note the bright second headlight (Mars oscillating) above the two-bulb sealed beam light in the normal position. (John Rehor, Jay Williams Collection)

The Alpha and Omega of Lima NKP Berkshires. No. 715, the first S-1 at left and No. 779, the last S-3 are both eastbound at GC Tower, Vermillion, Ohio on January 27, 1957. (John Rehor Photo, Jay Williams Collection)

NKP Hudsons

One other class of NKP locomotives came from Lima and fit the Super Power mode. These were the four 4-6-4 Hudsons of 1929. Certainly not a part of the NKP's major thrust for new power, which pertained to its main business, hauling fast freight, and ordered before the Advisory Mechanical Committee had much to say, the four new Hudsons came in late 1929 to continue a modernization of NKP passenger power begun in 1927 when 4-6-4 Nos. 170-173 were delivered by Alco's Brooks Works. It's interesting to note that they arrived at about the same time as the NYC Hudsons, which gave the type its name. They were much needed to power NKP's passenger trains. NKP had a limited passenger service which was hauled mainly by 1922-era Pacifics (from both Lima and Alco) as well as some 4-6-0s. However, the road wanted to increase its competitiveness in passenger traffic in the last great days of the 1920s, and ordered the additional four 4-6-4s. They were among the lightest of all 4-6-4s ever built, at 314,000 lbs. engine weight. They had 73-inch drivers, 25x26 cylinders, but sported the 4-wheel trailing truck mainly as a device to allow for lighter axle loads rather than to carry a much larger firebox. To round out the 4-6-4 fleet Lima built the final four in 1929.

In appearance they hardy look like a Super Power locomotive, and they certainly are on the margin of whether or not they should be so classified because their roughly 66 square foot grade area was not in the same league as most locomotives with the 4-wheel trailer. However, adhering to the first criteria for inclusion in this book, that of possessing a 4-wheel trailing truck, they are reviewed herewith.

Eventually the boiler pressures were raised from 215 to 225 psi. Arrival of the famous "Blue Bird" Alco PA diesels doomed the Hudsons on NKP passenger trains in late 1947 and early 1948.

Above: Lima broadside of No. 177 the last of four Hudsons that it built for NKP in 1929 just does not give the impression of a Super Power locomotive, either from the appearance of the firebox, size of boiler, or size of tender. (Lima, TLC Collection)

BUILT FOR			RAILROAD CLASS		ROAD NUMBERS		LIMA ORDER NUMBER		
NICKEL PLATE ROAD			L-1B		174-177		1114		
DELIVERED	174-177: NOVEMBER, 1929					CONSTRUCTION NUMBERS		7399-7402	
WHEEL ARRANGEMENT	DRIVING WHEEL DIAMETER		CYLINDERS		BOILER		FIREBOX		
			DIAMETER	STROKE	DIAMETER	PRESSURE	LENGTH	WIDTH	GRATE AREA
4-6-4	73"		25"	26"	83 1/16"	215 p.s.i.	114 1/8"	84¼"	66.7 SQ.FT.
WHEEL BASE			TRACTIVE POWER		FACTOR OF ADHESION		TUBES AND FLUES		
DRIVING	ENGINE	ENGINE AND TENDER	MAIN CYLINDERS				NUMBER	DIAMETER	LENGTH
13' 0"	37' 9"	73' 7¾"	40,680 lbs.		4.32		224 45	2¼" 5½"	20'
AVERAGE WEIGHT IN WORKING ORDER, POUNDS					HEATING SURFACES, SQUARE FEET				
ON DRIVERS	TRUCK	TRAILER		TOTAL ENGINE	TUBES AND FLUES	FIREBOX & COMB. CHAM.	ARCH TUBES & SYPHONS	TOTAL	SUPERHEATER
		FRONT AXLE	REAR AXLE						
176,000	53,500	34,000	50,500	314,000	3,917	232	70	4,219	1,045
TENDER									
TYPE	FUEL	WATER	WEIGHT, FULLY LOADED						
8 WHEEL	16 TONS	11,000 GALS	206,200 LBS.						

L-1b class NKP 4-6-4 No. 174 is pictured here on Train No. 7, The Westerner, at Chicago's suburban Englewood, Illinois, station July 23, 1943. Its face looks very much like NKP Berkshires: centered headlight/number board, high bell, shielded pumps. The appearance is very pleasing, but it simply doesn't have the bulk expected when one speaks of Super Power. (C. T. Felstead, Jay Williams Collection)

A nice broadside view of L-1b No. 175 with experimental smoke deflectors applied, at Rocky River, Ohio, July 2, 1956. It will be noted that it is in freight service, long after being bumped from passenger trains by the Bluebird Alco PA diesels. (Phil Horning Photo).

NKP Train No. 5, the Nickel Plate Limited, *in East Cleveland May 6, 1934, with a varied 9-car consist. (Andrew Hritz Photo, Jay Williams Collection)*

Lima builder photo of the N Class, new in 1937. The 22-ton/22,000-gallon tender riding on its 6-wheel trucks looks and in fact essentially was the same as the NKP 2-8-4 tender. One change from the NKP 2-8-4 design was the slatted pilot whereas NKP used the standard boiler-tube type. Another change with respect to the NKP engines was the addition of a trailing truck booster on the last five engines of this class, Nos. 1211 through 1215, evident in this photo by the vertical steam exhaust pipe under the first digit of the cab number, and also by the space it fills behind the trailing truck. (Lima Photo, TLC Collection)

The N-1 class looks the same as the N-class with the minor exceptions of some piping ahead of the steam dome and the addition of a fifth outlet from the sand dome. None of this class were equipped with boosters, most readily seen by comparing the empty space behind the trailing truck, as compared to booster equipped No. 1213 above. (Lima Photo, TLC Collection)

A quick study of the profile here shows that the N-2 class reversed the positions of the steam dome and sand box. The exact reasoning for this isn't clear, unless it was to get better distribution of the sand in front of the drivers by moving the storage forward. Just as with the class N group, five of these locomotives, Nos. 1235 through 1239, were equipped with boosters. (Lima Photo, TLC Collection)

The Pere Marquette Railway's tracks were mainly in Michigan and Ontario, with connections into Chicago, and into Wisconsin via railroad car ferry across Lake Michigan. It was an amalgam of many small railroads, and was never strong until the rise of the automobile industry in Michigan. It was acquired by the Van Sweringens in 1924, the year after they captured the Chesapeake & Ohio, because it was thought that the PM would supply a good outlet for C&O-originated coal to be used in the rising automotive industry, and likewise could supply a good flow of completed vehicles to C&O for forwarding to other railroads. This connection was available via the C&O-controlled Hocking Valley Railway between Columbus and Toledo (merged into C&O after 1930).

PM's motive power at the time consisted of mainly 2-8-0 and 2-8-2 types as well as some 2-10-2s for freight service, none of remarkable dimensions or capabilities. However they were capable of carrying the traffic offered at reasonably good speeds over the mainlines of the company, which were essentially without any long heavy grades or other adverse topographical features.

By the mid-1930s, with the Depression financial problems abating and the automotive industry regaining strength, management recognized the need to modernize PM's motive power. PM's best locomotives were 2-8-2s built between 1913 and 1918, with ten more that were delivered in 1927. Additionally, 17 lumbering 2-10-2 Santa Fe types were also available for the heaviest work.

Since PM was under control of the Van Sweringen's Advisory Mechanical Committee (see page 57) its policies were regulated by that entity. After carefully studying PM's traffic, it was decided that the 2-8-4 would be the best application. After all, PM was not unlike the NKP in its topography, and needed to move mainly merchandise freight at relatively quick speeds. The 2-8-4s purchased for NKP in 1934 had proven their worth and it was a natural fit for PM's conditions and traffic. Looking back to the 2-8-4s of the Erie (from which the NKP locomotives ultimately descended) was another good example of a road with similar conditions to the PM, and the 2-8-4s had improved conditions there very effectively.

AMC's mechanical engineers designed a locomotive that could handle PM traffic with appropriate speed, and increase the average ton-miles per train over the whole line, and an order was placed Lima for fifteen. Given PM Class designation "N" they arrived September-November 1937, and went to work on PM's mainline between Detroit and Chicago via Grand Rapids, and between Toledo and Saginaw, all of which were lines built heavily enough to accommodate the big new locomotives.

The last five of the N-class were equipped with boosters, adding 14,400 pounds of starting tractive effort, to be used for the heaviest work, and probably for locomotives assigned to the Grand Rapids-Chicago mainline with its heavy grade.

The N-class was so satisfactory and the increase in business by 1940 so marked, that PM needed additional Berkshires and 12 more, classed N-1, were received in late 1941, just in time to help handle the huge war-time traffic that came to PM because of its vital position serving the automotive centers where so much war materiel was built.

To further help with the accelerating traffic an additional twelve 2-8-4s were delivered in 1944, classed N-2, five of which had boosters. The big Berkshires had no problem in handing 3,500-ton trains through the rolling Michigan countryside, and kept the road humming during the war years.

Following the war, the automotive traffic didn't diminish. In fact it accelerated when the pent-up demand for private and commercial vehicles caused by the war exploded. PM and its 2-8-4s were ideally positioned to handle this with speed and efficiency. However, the diesel was on the horizon, and Pere Marquette was merged into C&O in 1947. Though C&O was still committed to "coal fired" locomotives, it was not adverse to buying diesels for the former PM lines, and this only accelerated once the old C&O fell into line and began buying diesels for its Virginia-West Virginia-Kentucky-Ohio lines. The entire PM was dieselized by mid-1951, and the 2-8-4s were surplus. Because power was still needed on the as yet not completely dieselized southern lines, a number of the PM Berkshires went south, several working out of the giant Russell, Kentucky, terminal, and others out of the Clifton Forge, Virginia, where they were used exactly like the C&O K-4 class 2-8-4s, which they resembled in most ways. They had a last hurrah until enough diesels arrived to displace them even there. With nowhere else to go, they were retired and scrapped.

After the C&O merger some of the PM 2-8-4s were assigned C&O numbers in the 2600-series. Some were repainted with C&O lettering and the new numbers, but others retained their PM scheme until retirement. Once the 39 PM 2-8-4s were merged with the 90 C&O locomotives of this type, this gave C&O a total of 119 of the 2-8-4 type, the most ever operated by any railroad.

A good ¾ view of PM 1229 marks it as an AMC-designed locomotive from the road name on the sandbox to the centered headlight, high bell, jacketed pumps up front, feedwater heater --ahead of the stack, spacious cab, and large tender riding on 6-wheel trucks. (Lima Photo, TLC Collection)

Lima detail photo shows the firebox and cab area of No. 1229 in April 1944. Note that the firebox has been lagged and jacketed. (Lima Photo, TLC Collection)

Head-on smoke box view of PM 1222. The number board was a steel plate with separate numerals bolted on. (Lima photo, TLC Collection)

PERE MARQUETTE CLASS N NO. 1201-1215   ORDER NO. 1143

DELIVERED	1201-1205, 1211-1213: SEPTEMBER, 1937; 1214-1215: OCTOBER, 1937; 1206-1210: NOVEMBER, 1937				CONSTRUCTION NUMBERS		7737-7751		
WHEEL ARRANGEMENT		DRIVING WHEEL DIAMETER	CYLINDERS		BOILER		FIREBOX		
2-8-4		69"	DIAMETER	STROKE	DIAMETER	PRESSURE	LENGTH	WIDTH	GRATE AREA
			26"	34"	87 $^{15}/_{16}$"	245 p.s.i.	135 $^{1}/_{16}$"	96¼"	90.3 SQ.FT.
WHEEL BASE			TRACTIVE POWER		FACTOR OF ADHESION		TUBES AND FLUES		
DRIVING	ENGINE	ENGINE AND TENDER	MAIN CYLINDERS WITH BOOSTER (5 ENGINES)				NUMBER	DIAMETER	LENGTH
18' 3"	42' 0"	87' 8¾"	69,350 lbs. 83,750 lbs.		4.01		74 202	2¼" 3½"	19'
AVERAGE WEIGHT IN WORKING ORDER, POUNDS					HEATING SURFACES, SQUARE FEET				
ON DRIVERS	TRUCK	TRAILER		TOTAL ENGINE	TUBES AND FLUES	FIREBOX & COMB. CHAM.	ARCH TUBES & SYPHONS	TOTAL	SUPERHEATER
		FRONT AXLE	REAR AXLE						
278,000	48,000	53,500	66,000	455,500	4,323	343	119	4,785	1,932
TENDER									
TYPE	FUEL	WATER	WEIGHT, FULLY LOADED						
12 WHEEL	22 TONS	22,000 GALS	358,000 LBS.						

NOTE: ENGINES 1211-1215 WERE EQUIPPED WITH BOOSTERS, AND MATCHED THE SPECIFICATIONS GIVEN ABOVE. ENGINES 1201-1210 DID NOT HAVE BOOSTERS, AND HAD SOMEWHAT LESS WEIGHT ON THE TRAILER AND LESS WEIGHT OVERALL, SIMILAR TO ENGINES 1216-1227, DESCRIBED BELOW.

PERE MARQUETTE CLASS N-1 NO. 1216-1227   ORDER NO. 1155

DELIVERED	1216-1224: OCTOBER, 1941; 1225-1227: NOVEMBER, 1942				CONSTRUCTION NUMBERS		7830-7841		
WHEEL ARRANGEMENT		DRIVING WHEEL DIAMETER	CYLINDERS		BOILER		FIREBOX		
2-8-4		69"	DIAMETER	STROKE	DIAMETER	PRESSURE	LENGTH	WIDTH	GRATE AREA
			26"	34"	87 $^{15}/_{16}$"	245 p.s.i.	135 $^{1}/_{16}$"	96¼"	90.3 SQ.FT.
WHEEL BASE			TRACTIVE POWER		FACTOR OF ADHESION		TUBES AND FLUES		
DRIVING	ENGINE	ENGINE AND TENDER	MAIN CYLINDERS				NUMBER	DIAMETER	LENGTH
18' 3"	42' 0"	87' 8¾"	69,350 lbs.		4.01		73 202	2¼" 3½"	19'
AVERAGE WEIGHT IN WORKING ORDER, POUNDS					HEATING SURFACES, SQUARE FEET				
ON DRIVERS	TRUCK	TRAILER		TOTAL ENGINE	TUBES AND FLUES	FIREBOX & COMB. CHAM.	ARCH TUBES & SYPHONS	TOTAL	SUPERHEATER
		FRONT AXLE	REAR AXLE						
277,600	50,900	56,000	58,000	442,500	4,311	344	122	4,777	1,932
TENDER									
TYPE	FUEL	WATER	WEIGHT, WEIGHT, $^{2}/_{3}$ LOAD						
12 WHEEL	22 TONS	22,000 GALS	284,800 LBS.						

PERE MARQUETTE CLASS N-2 NO. 1228-1239   ORDER NO. 1180

DELIVERED	1235: MARCH, 1944; 1228-1229, 1237-1239: APRIL, 1944; 1230-1234: MAY, 1944				CONSTRUCTION NUMBERS		8457-8472		
WHEEL ARRANGEMENT		DRIVING WHEEL DIAMETER	CYLINDERS		BOILER		FIREBOX		
2-8-4		69"	DIAMETER	STROKE	DIAMETER	PRESSURE	LENGTH	WIDTH	GRATE AREA
			26"	34"	87 $^{15}/_{16}$"	245 p.s.i.	135 $^{1}/_{16}$"	96¼"	90.3 SQ.FT.
WHEEL BASE			TRACTIVE POWER		FACTOR OF ADHESION		TUBES AND FLUES		
DRIVING	ENGINE	ENGINE AND TENDER	MAIN CYLINDERS WITH BOOSTER (5 ENGINES)				NUMBER	DIAMETER	LENGTH
18' 3"	42' 0"	87' 8¾"	69,350 lbs. 83,450 lbs.		4.01		73 202	2¼" 3½"	19'
AVERAGE WEIGHT IN WORKING ORDER, POUNDS					HEATING SURFACES, SQUARE FEET				
ON DRIVERS	TRUCK	TRAILER		TOTAL ENGINE	TUBES AND FLUES	FIREBOX & COMB. CHAM.	ARCH TUBES & SYPHONS	TOTAL	SUPERHEATER
		FRONT AXLE	REAR AXLE						
277,600	50,500	60,100	67,500	456,100	4,311	344	122	4,777	1,932
TENDER									
TYPE	FUEL	WATER	WEIGHT, WEIGHT, FULLY LOADED						
12 WHEEL	22 TONS	22,000 GALS	365,300 LBS.						

NOTE: ENGINES 1235-1239 WERE EQUIPPED WITH BOOSTERS, AND MATCHED THE SPECIFICATIONS GIVEN ABOVE. ENGINES 1228-1234 DID NOT HAVE BOOSTERS, AND HAD SOMEWHAT LESS WEIGHT ON THE TRAILER AND LESS WEIGHT OVERALL, SIMILAR TO ENGINES 1216-1227, DESCRIBED ABOVE.

PM applied large 22-ton/22,000-gallon tenders almost exactly the same a those used on NKP 2-8-4s. PM was the only railroad named for Roman Catholic priest. Actually it is not, it takes its name from the old Flint & Pere Marquette of the late 1800s. At that time the town now known as Ludington, on the shores of Lake Michigan was called Pere Marquette (after the French priest-explorer), so it really was a geographic designation. (Lima Photo, TLC Collection)

Front of a PM N-2 class 2-8-4 shows the road name on the sandbox clearly in its new position ahead of the steam dome. Lima's distinctive diamond-shaped builder's plate is quite clear in this very sharp photo. This was a photo made by the Lima photographer for study in the engineering department. (Lima Photo, TLC Collection)

N-1 class No. 1221 has a solid oil tanker train arriving at Grand Rapids in this 1943 scene showing part of the work these super locomotives did during the busy and specialized traffic era of the war. (C&O Ry. Photo, C&O Hist. Soc. Coll.)

N-1 No. 1229 poses for a dramatic publicity photo to be used in annual reports and other advertising. (C&O Ry. Photo, C&O Hist. Soc. Coll. Image No. 5145)

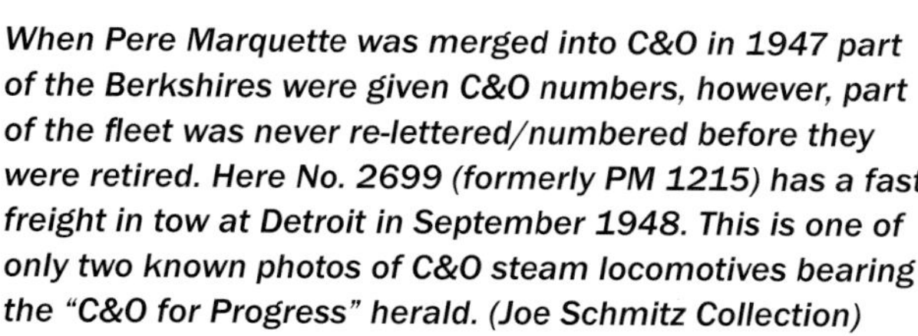

When Pere Marquette was merged into C&O in 1947 part of the Berkshires were given C&O numbers, however, part of the fleet was never re-lettered/numbered before they were retired. Here No. 2699 (formerly PM 1215) has a fast freight in tow at Detroit in September 1948. This is one of only two known photos of C&O steam locomotives bearing the "C&O for Progress" herald. (Joe Schmitz Collection)

Left and right broadsides of RF&P 2-8-4 No. 574 new at Lima. This was a handsome locomotive decorated with the Richmond-Washington RF&P logo, pin-striping on the cab, sandbox, and tender, and graphite smokebox. The spoked drivers were also pin striped. The number plates under the cab were brass bolted to the cab side. The boiler was clean with the sand pipes encased. Note, too, that unlike most of the Van Sweringen design 2-8-4s, these engines had inside bearing pilot trucks, enhancing their gracefull looks. If any Super Power locomotive exemplified the "Georgian" look in locomotives, these did. (Lima Photos, Kevin Kohls Collection)

Close-up of the huge 25-ton/22,000 gallon tender showing the pin-striping, lettering, and logo. RF&P had an understated, elegant southern style about it. Although not named as were the 4-8-4s, the 2-8-4s still had that patrician look. (Lima Photo, Kevin Kohls Collection)

Opposite: From this view of the 574 one can easily compare it to the contemporary NKP 2-8-4s after which it was patterned. (Lima Photo, Kevin Kohls Collection)

The RF&P's main purpose was as a bridge line running north-south for 113 miles between Richmond, Virginia, and Alexandria, Virginia (Washington, D. C.). It was responsible for forwarding trains operating to and from the South by the Atlantic Coast Line and Seaboard Air Line, connecting them to the Pennsylvania, Baltimore & Ohio, Chesapeake & Ohio, and the whole northeastern grid via the large Potomac yard at Alexandria. It had no branches of consequence and little on-line local traffic. It was a "racetrack" of well maintained, high quality double track between the two cities and really served as the link of north and south. Because of it the other railroads never built their own lines between Richmond and Washington. It was owned jointly by PRR, B&O, C&O, Southern, and the Commonwealth of Virginia.

The overall motive power policy of the RF&P from the outset was to buy dual-service locomotives. Because of the nature of its bridge-line traffic, coupled with the density of that traffic, freight and passenger trains had to move at comparable speeds. RF&P had to forward all the heavy premier New York-Florida passenger trains, including seasonal business, that operated over SAL and ACL.

By the early part of the 20th Century RF&P was buying 4-6-0 Ten Wheelers, but very quickly began using heavier 4-6-2 Pacifics and between 1904 and 1927 acquired more than 60 of the type. The last RF&P Pacific types, from Baldwin, were among the heaviest of the type ever built. In 1924-25 RF&P finally bought some heavier locomotives in the form of four Mountain types which were used extensively in both fast freight and passenger work. Then Super Power came in 1937 in the form of five 4-8-4s from Baldwin. Their proportions were too large for them to enter Washington over the Long Bridge over the Potomac from Alexandria, and they were therefore used exclusively in freight service between Richmond and Potomac yard in Alexandria. Starting in 1938 and ending in 1944 Baldwin built 22 more 4-8-4s, this time with specifications that allowed them to serve as dual purpose power.

This situation placed RF&P in a good position to handle the heavy traffic that it was given at both ends of its short run, but once World War II traffic patterns emerged, the railroad found itself overtaxed. With war-time limitations in effect on new locomotive designs, and with the need for quick delivery paramount, RF&P turned to Lima for the first time, and simply asked it to duplicate the Nickel Plate 2-8-4 Berkshire types that the company was producing at the time. This expedient allowed quick delivery so that the 10 new locomotives could get to work as soon as possible. Thus the final product, RF&P's 2-8-4s, came out of Lima looking very much like Van Sweringen Berkshires (see earlier treatment in this book).

RICHMOND, FREDERICKSBURG & POTOMAC NO. 571-580 ORDER NO. 1168			
DELIVERED	571: JANUARY, 1943; 572-579: FEBRUARY, 1943; 580: MARCH, 1943	CONSTRUCTION NUMBERS	8023-8032

WHEEL ARRANGEMENT	DRIVING WHEEL DIAMETER	CYLINDERS		BOILER		FIREBOX		
		DIAMETER	STROKE	DIAMETER	PRESSURE	LENGTH	WIDTH	GRATE AREA
2-8-4	69"	25"	34"	87 15/16"	245 p.s.i.	135 1/16"	96¼"	90.3 SQ.FT.

WHEEL BASE			TRACTIVE POWER	FACTOR OF ADHESION		TUBES AND FLUES		
DRIVING	ENGINE	ENGINE AND TENDER	MAIN CYLINDERS			NUMBER	DIAMETER	LENGTH
18' 3"	42' 0"	94' 0¾"	64,100 lbs.	4.23		73 202	2¼" 3½"	19'

AVERAGE WEIGHT IN WORKING ORDER, POUNDS					HEATING SURFACES, SQUARE FEET				
ON DRIVERS	TRUCK	TRAILER FRONT AXLE	TRAILER REAR AXLE	TOTAL ENGINE	TUBES AND FLUES	FIREBOX & COMB. CHAM.	ARCH TUBES & SYPHONS	TOTAL	SUPERHEATER
270,900	50,300	51,200	60,800	433,200	4,311	344	117	4,772	1,932

TENDER			
TYPE	FUEL	WATER	*WEIGHT, 2/3 LOAD*
12 WHEEL	25 TONS	22,000 GALS	303,400

They were given a rating of 3,200 tons northbound and 2,500 tons southbound over the RF&P.

Although an order of only ten locomotives seems small, it must be considered that they were powering trains over a fairly short run of 113 miles at reasonably high speeds, so they could make multiple trips on quick turn-arounds. Their large 25 ton/22,000 gallon tenders made it possible to run through the entire route without stopping for fuel or water. These fine looking locomotives did superb work during the latter half of the war and were the principal freight locomotive after the war until RF&P began buying diesels. By the end of the war RF&P had 72 road locomo-

Two of the 2-8-4s rest from their work at the Potomac Yard roundhouse radial tracks July 4, 1946. (L. W. Rice Photo, TLC Collection)

tives whose tractive power was 50% greater than those in operation in before.

Diesels first arrived for switching work at Acca yard in 1942 and at Potomac yard in 1946. It was not until 1949 that RF&P started its campaign to dieselize road service. It should be noted that many SAL and ACL passenger trains operating over RF&P with diesel power had been run through between Richmond and Washington without changing to RF&P locomotives since before the war.

EMD E8s for the passengers arrived in 1949 followed by F7s and FP7s in 1949 and 1950 and a few GP7s in 1950 and 1953. All steam was shortly gone, with the last steam run on January 4, 1954 by a 4-8-4, the 2-8-4s having been retired the year before.

Head-on view of No. 576 in service, with the usual Lima face: centered headlight and number plate, shielded pumps, and high bell. The automatic Train Control notice was lettered on the pilot deck device. (L. W. Rice, TLC Collection)

Bulky and massive, yet tasteful and elegant in appearance, 571 pauses under the Potomac yard coaling station March 20, 1948. Note that overfire jets or smoke consumers had been added to the firebox side by this time. (L W. Rice Photo, TLC Collection)

VIRGININAN CLASS AG NO. 900-907 ORDER NO. 1190

DELIVERED	900: MARCH, 1944; 901-904: APRIL, 1944; 905-906: MAY, 1944; 907: JUNE, 1944	CONSTRUCTION NUMBERS	8859-8866

WHEEL ARRANGEMENT	DRIVING WHEEL DIAMETER	CYLINDERS		BOILER		FIREBOX		
		DIAMETER	STROKE	DIAMETER	PRESSURE	LENGTH	WIDTH	GRATE AREA
2-6-6-6	67"	22 ½"	33"	100 $^{9}/_{16}$"	260 p.s.i.	180"	108¼"	135.3 SQ.FT.

WHEEL BASE			TRACTIVE POWER	FACTOR OF ADHESION		TUBES AND FLUES		
DRIVING	ENGINE	ENGINE AND TENDER	MAIN CYLINDERS			NUMBER	DIAMETER	LENGTH
34' 8"	62' 6"	112' 11"	110,200 lbs.	4.49		58 219	2¼" 4"	23'

AVERAGE WEIGHT IN WORKING ORDER, POUNDS				HEATING SURFACES, SQUARE FEET				
ON DRIVERS	TRUCK	TRAILER	TOTAL ENGINE	TUBES AND FLUES	FIREBOX & COMB. CHAM.	ARCH TUBES & SYPHONS	TOTAL	SUPERHEATER
495,000	67,500	190,500	753,000	6,033	600	162	6,795	2,922

TENDER			
TYPE	FUEL	WATER	*WEIGHT, $^{2}/_{3}$ LOAD*
14 WHEEL	25 TONS	26,500 GALS	351,500

VIRGINIAN CLASS BA NO. 505-509 ORDER NO. 1194

DELIVERED	505-506: JUNE, 1946; 507-509: JULY, 1946	CONSTRUCTION NUMBERS	9104-9111

WHEEL ARRANGEMENT	DRIVING WHEEL DIAMETER	CYLINDERS		BOILER		FIREBOX		
		DIAMETER	STROKE	DIAMETER	PRESSURE	LENGTH	WIDTH	GRATE AREA
2-8-4	69"	26"	34"	87 $^{15}/_{16}$"	245 p.s.i.	135 $^{1}/_{16}$"	96¼"	90.3 SQ.FT.

WHEEL BASE			TRACTIVE POWER	FACTOR OF ADHESION		TUBES AND FLUES		
DRIVING	ENGINE	ENGINE AND TENDER	MAIN CYLINDERS			NUMBER	DIAMETER	LENGTH
18' 3"	42' 0"	93' 2"	69,350 lbs.	4.26		73 202	2¼" 3½"	19'

AVERAGE WEIGHT IN WORKING ORDER, POUNDS					HEATING SURFACES, SQUARE FEET				
ON DRIVERS	TRUCK	TRAILER		TOTAL ENGINE	TUBES AND FLUES	FIREBOX & COMB. CHAM.	ARCH TUBES & SYPHONS	TOTAL	SUPERHEATER
		FRONT AXLE	REAR AXLE						
295,600	46,000	57,500	61,300	460,400	4,308	344	122	4,774	1,932

TENDER			
TYPE	FUEL	WATER	*WEIGHT, $^{2}/_{3}$ LOAD*
12 WHEEL	21 TONS	25,000 GALS	326,800

The Virginian Railway is peculiar among railways. It came very late, having been completed in 1909, and it was built with almost a single purpose: to carry coal from southern West Virginia to piers at Norfolk, Virginia, from which it could be shipped mainly to markets in the northeastern U. S. and overseas. It was built in direct and blatant competition with the two larger railways that were already well established in this traffic, the Chesapeake & Ohio and the Norfolk & Western. Those much larger lines concentrated on coal, but had much through freight and high class passenger business as well. However, the Virginian had no passenger service to speak off, providing some coach-only accommodation trains along its main line and branches, and didn't even provide any sleeping or dining services, and had little through freight.

Because of the Virginian's heavy grades out of the coal fields, it entered the Mallet compound articulated locomotive market early, buying 2-6-6-0s, 2-8-8-2s, 2-10-10-2s and an experimental 2-8-8-8-4! When the idea of electrification came into mainstream railroad thinking in the early decades of the 20th Century, neighbor N&W electrified a portion of its heaviest grades west of Bluefield, W. Va., and noting its success, Virginian did more, and in 1924 electrified its entire mainline between Mullens, W. Va., and Roanoke, Va. – over 133 miles. No longer were hugely powerful steam locomotives needed to challenge the Allegheny and Blue Ridge grades, and the big compounds were put to work on the coal branches and in assembling coal trains along the main line. On the non-electrified line east of Roanoke some of the smaller Mallets were used, as well as a fleet of sturdy Mikado 2-8-2s. This situation continued until the war-time traffic, and a change in executive officers occurred. In 1942 George D. Brooke lost his position as president of the C&O. He moved over to become chairman of the Virginian, and brought Frank Beale (who had been a C&O vice president) with him, who was installed at VGN president. They brought with them the C&O's designs for Lima Super Power 2-8-4s and 2-6-6-6s.

Opposite Top: Lima broadside of VGN AG class 2-6-6-6 No. 900 a virtual duplicate of C&O's. As was later discovered, however, it was considerably lighter than C&O version. C&O and VGN are the only railroads ever to have a locomotive with a 6-wheel trailing truck to support a simply monstrous firebox. (Lima Photo, Allen County Historical Society collection)

Opposite Lower: Lima broadside of VGN 505 when compared with C&O K-4 on page ____ of this book, one will see that it is a duplicate is every regard except the moving of the sand box farther back on the boiler, and enclosing it and the steam dome in the same casing. (Lima Photo, Kevin Kohls Collection)

Since VGN didn't need new, bigger, more powerful steam for the mountains, they wanted more powerful steam that could haul trains on flatter land at higher speeds and deliver great horsepower at speed. The C&O 2-8-4 and 2-6-6-6 were the ideal machines for this purpose. In late 1944 Virginian ordered five 2-8-4s that were essentially direct copies of C&O K-4 class 2-8-4 Kanawha types. VGN classed them "BA" and called them Blue Ridge types. They took VGN road numbers 505-509 when they arrived in mid-1946. The eight 2-6-6-6s that VGN ordered in late 1944 were copies of C&O's H-8 class engines and they were the only 2-6-6-6s built outside C&O's huge fleet of 60. Given class AG and road numbers 900-907 they arrived in mid-1944 in time to handle a lot of late WWII traffic and post-war traffic.

Both the BAs and the AGs were used exclusively between Roanoke and Norfolk through the easy grades of the Virginia Piedmont and Tidewater, with the BAs usually in regular freight service as well a coal trains, and the AGs almost exclusively in coal train service, hauling huge trains east on an essentially down-grade line to the sea. The AGs weighed, according to official Lima statistics, 753,000 pounds engine weight, heavier than the C&O's, but it was later discovered that the C&O engine had been improperly weighed and they actually tipped the sales at 778,000 pounds, giving them the title of the heaviest steam locomotive ever built.

Like neighbors N&W and C&O, Virginian didn't contemplate diesels as quickly as most railroads, and when it dieselized it bought all Fairbanks Morse units, the only railroad to have an all-FM fleet (except for one engine, actually).

VGN began buying the FM diesel units to replace steam in the coal fields and on the mainline east of Roanoke and by 1955 steam was through.

Although the Virginian had no financial or operational connection with the Van Sweringen railroads and their Advisory Mechanical Committee (see page 57), these locomotives were direct copies of AMC designs and therefore fit right in with the AMC design story.

Resting at Roanoke on September 15, 1949, all the parts and details of AG Class No. 905 are quite visible because of a coating of sand dust and road grime. The AGs were used to speed trains across Virginia from Roanoke to Norfolk, displacing old Mallets. (Jay Williams Collection)

Left side view of VGN 902, another of the gargantuan AG class 2-6-6-6s. At Sewell's Point in 1947. (Jay Williams Collection)

No. 900 rolls a coal train through Suffolk, Virginia, past a westbound passenger train. Note the white running gear from heavy sanding. (Joe Collias Photo, Jay Williams Collection)

A shinny new No. 505 poses at Lima having just emerged from the shop. Except for the lettering one would identify it as a C&O K-4 class right down to the oval number board and low-mounted headlight. (Lima Photo, Kevin Kohls Collection)

BA Class No. 507 is rolling empty hoppers west in Norfolk County, Virginia December 23, 1951 with a superb show of white steam exhaust. (H. Reid Photo, TLC Collection)

In its last months of operation, at Sewell's Point piers in Norfolk, VGN 505 is still working hard for its owners, but about to be bumped aside by Fairbanks Morse opposed-piston diesels. (Jay Williams Collection)

Above: VGN AG 2-6-6-6 No. 904 with a westbound train of empty coal cars arriving at Roanoke, Va. circa 1953. Note the overhead wires for the VGN's electrified lines, which extend west from this point. The VGN's Roanoke station is in the background.

Below: BA Class 2-8-4 No. 506 at speed with a freight train at Norfolk, Va. in November, 1953. While the VGN didn't handle a large amount of manifest freight, what they did they hustled right along, as shown by the nice plume of steam from the locomotive.

(Both photos by H. Reid, TLC Collection)

Lima builder's photo of L&N class M-1 2-8-4. (Lima photo, Allen County Historical Society Collection)

Dirty with road grime and sand dust No. 1991, is at DeCoursey yard in 1951. No. 1991 was the last M-1 and almost the last Lima Super Power locomotive; only NKP's No. 779 was completed later. (W. Krawiec Photo, Jay Williams Collection)

LOUISVILLE & NASHVILLE CLASS M-1 NO. 1970-1991 ORDER NO. 1208									
DELIVERED		1970-1973: JANUARY, 1949; 1974-1978: FEBRUARY, 1949; 1979-1982: MARCH, 1949; 1983-1989: APRIL, 1949; 1990-1991: MAY, 1949					CONSTRUCTION NUMBERS		9349-9370
WHEEL ARRANGEMENT		DRIVING WHEEL DIAMETER	CYLINDERS		BOILER		FIREBOX		
2-8-4		69"	DIAMETER	STROKE	DIAMETER	PRESSURE	LENGTH	WIDTH	GRATE AREA
			25"	32"	88"	265 p.s.i.	135 $^{3}/_{32}$"	96$^{3}/_{16}$"	90.2 SQ.FT.
WHEEL BASE			TRACTIVE POWER		FACTOR OF ADHESION		TUBES AND FLUES		
DRIVING	ENGINE	ENGINE AND TENDER	MAIN CYLINDERS WITH BOOSTER				NUMBER	DIAMETER	LENGTH
18' 3"	42' 4"	93' 8"	65,290 lbs. 79,290		4.10		62 202	2¼" 3½"	19'
AVERAGE WEIGHT IN WORKING ORDER, POUNDS					HEATING SURFACES, SQUARE FEET				
ON DRIVERS	TRUCK	TRAILER		TOTAL ENGINE	TUBES AND FLUES	FIREBOX & COMB. CHAM.	SYPHONS	TOTAL	SUPERHEATER
		FRONT AXLE	REAR AXLE						
267,500	52,900	61,300	66,400	448,100	4,190	338	125	4,653	1,908
TENDER									
TYPE	FUEL	WATER	*WEIGHT, $^{2}/_{3}$ LOAD*						
12 WHEEL	25 TONS	22,000 GALS	308,900						

The L&N was a sizeable railroad that had principal lines serving Kentucky, Tennessee, Alabama, and other mains that connected to Chicago, Cincinnati, and St. Louis through Indiana and Illinois, and New Orleans through Mississippi. It was an important coal hauler, with numerous highly productive branches in the coal fields of Kentucky, Tennessee, and western Virginia. Controlled itself by the Atlantic Coast Line, it controlled the Clinchfield Railroad which also tapped important coal resources in the Appalachian range.

Although L&N certainly had the traffic and terrain that would have required articulated locomotives on most railroads, it never ventured into this area of motive power, preferring to have smaller rigid wheelbase locomotives and using them as doubleheaders and helpers as needed.

L&N also had a huge shop facility in Louisville in which it not only refurbished and rebuilt locomotives, but actually built many from scratch rather than buying them from commercial builders, much as Norfolk & Western did at Roanoke. The motive power fleet consisted of a large number of 2-8-0 Consolidations as well as about 350 2-8-2 Mikados (about half of which were heavy USRA types) for freight service, while Pacifics were standard passenger power.

However, with the advent of World War II, new power was needed. Additionally it was time that L&N considered what its future motive power policy would be. They sampled some switcher diesels before the war, but in 1941 with the need to get new power quickly, L&N leaped into Super Power by ordering from Baldwin 20 2-8-4 types, based on the design of the Van Sweringen Berkshires used on the NKP and PM, which arrived in 1942. They were given L&N Class M-1 and road numbers 1950-1969. Their performance was superb and L&N was more than happy with them throughout the balance of the war and even following.

Of course, the years following the war were the age of the diesel, and although L&N was very much in the camp of the coal-hauling roads that wanted to maintain steam power as long as possible, it too decided to acquire diesels, including Alco and EMD road engines and road switchers. On the passenger side it started with EMD E6's in 1941 followed by E7s and E8s in the years after the war.

The 2-8-4s were assigned almost exclusively to lines in Kentucky where heavy coal traffic was their forte. They did a superb job at this, sometimes operating along with diesels on the same trains. When it would have seemed that L&N should have been buying more units to dieselize its coal fields main lines, instead in 1948 it ordered 22 more of the M-1s (nicknamed "Big Emmas"), this time from Lima (Nos. 1970-1991). This was the same year that Lima was building the last Super Power (for C&O and NKP). In fact, the L&N 2-8-4s were delivered in April/May 1949, at the same time that the last Lima NKP 2-8-4s were finished. It was just by chance that in May 1949 L&N M-1 No. 1991 was delivered right before NKP 779, which was the very last Lima Super Power engine. So, the Big Emmas were the penultimate Super Power built by Lima or anyone else, and within a few months of being the last commercially built steam for any American railroad. At the same time, L&N was buying diesels of several designs.

A study that appeared in *Railway Mechanical Engineer's* October 1949 issue, dealt with L&N's M-1 class as a whole (all 42 locomotives) since the Lima and the Baldwin locomotives were essentially the same, and were used in the same way. It was stated in this article that the M-1s with a 6-unit EMD F-unit pusher had increased tonnage ratings for coal trains from 6,500 to 9,500 tons on several divisions. The unusual steam-diesel combination was repeated on very few other railroads. The big engines were credited with increasing L&N's overall train miles per train hour from 14.9 in 1942 to 16.5 in 1949.

The M-1s were used primarily:

- Corbin to DeCoursey (major L&N yard south of Cincinnati), Ky. -185 miles

- Neon to DeCoursey, Ky. - 176 miles
- Loyall, Ky. to Corbin, Ky. - 67 miles (when not needed on first two runs).

On the Neon-DeCoursey run, the M-1s were changed, inspected and turned at Ravenna, Ky. It was reported that the average turn-around time for the M-1s servicing at a terminal was 1-½ hours, comparable with diesels. One thing L&N did to decrease maintenance costs and increase availability was to stop using run-of-mine coal and use washed and sized coal of from 3/8-inch minimum to 3-inch maximum. This cut down on stopped-up flues and slagging of flue sheets caused by slack coal. This also cut by 10.85 % the total coal consumption.

The diesel pushers were used on a 1.2% grade at Elkatawa Hill on both north and southbound trains. An M-1 leaving Neon with 9,500 ton train ran 153 miles to Ravenna where diesel pushers helped it up Elkatawa grade for 27 miles, cutting off at Winchester, and the single 2-8-4 took the train unassisted on the DeCoursey. On test, a single M-1 was able to take 11,056 tons Winchester-DeCoursey in 3 hours and 16 minutes.

But even for these efficient, powerful, late-date Super Power locomotives the time was up, and dieselization continued apace. All steam was gone by 1956, including the M-1s.

In fact, the last steam operation on L&N was M-1 No. 1950 (one of the Baldwins) when it brought a coal train into DeCoursey from Ravenna. The Lima M-1s had less than a decade, but had proven that Super Power reciprocating steam could compete alongside diesels, even as to availability, but it was fuel, maintenance, and infrastructure costs (shops, labor, track maintenance) that it couldn't overcome.

Lima ¾ left view of No. 1950, the first of the M-1 class it built, shows a very clean, modern appearance. The sandbox with its cased piping sets almost like a saddle in front of the steam dome. The stripes on the tender which carry over onto the cab and along the running board give the engine a distinctive look when viewed from the side and add a bit of styling in an era when diesel styling was a big part of locomotive design. The classification lights are mounted at the middle of the smokebox with a rather unusual arrangement. The Box pok drivers have a star painted in their centers! (Lima Photo, Kevin Kohls Collection)

Engineer's side of No. 1970, seen at a less steep angle, gives a better appreciation of the big locomotive. L&N was one of those roads which downplayed the road name and made the number the biggest part of the lettering scheme. The bolted covering just behind the stack is the location of the superheater header and front end throttle. (Lima Photo, Kevin Kohls Collection)

The one work that the M-1s handled their whole short lives was hauling heavy coal trains from the coal fields of eastern Kentucky to L&N's big yard at DeCoursey, Kentucky, just south of Cincinnati. They were too heavy for use on much of the road, and their power was best utilized on this, the heaviest (and most profitable) of L&N's traffic. Here No. 1982 is at Paris, Ky., on August 20, 1951. (Dick Acton, Sr. Photo, Jay Williams Collection)

Close-up of the front half of the engine. Many details of the locomotive can be seen here, including the two automatic lubricators, one just behind the cylinders and the other just below the power reverse, the Alco Type C power reverse, the Walschaerts valve gear, the air pumps, mounted just behind the pilot deck, and the decorative stars in the driver centers. On the top of the boiler, from front to back, can be seen the feedwater heater, the stack, the sandbox with its distinctive covers over the sanding valves, the steam dome, and the pop valve cluster. On the side of the smokebox is the characteristic diamond shaped Lima builders plate, and just above it the rectangular builders plate for the Type E superheater. (Lima Photo, Kevin Kohls Collection)

Smokebox view of No. 1970 displays the standard Lima Super Power image with some variations. Noticeable ones are the number on the headlight lens, the cylindrical air-pump shields, and the grill over the after-cooler coils. The prominent rivets also set these engines apart. The prominent steps on each side were enclosed for safety. The grill covers the air after cooler. (Lima Photo, Kevin Kohls Collection)

Southern Pacific

The Southern Pacific's 60 Lima-built semi-streamlined 4-8-4s are among the most well remembered locomotives that Lima built in its Super Power era. Except for twelve 2-8-8-4s, (and 10 second hand ex-B&M 2-8-4s) these were the only Lima-built Super Power on the SP.

Southern Pacific was a huge enterprise. It was the largest carrier for both freight and passenger traffic in California. Its mainlines challenged the torturous grades and snows of the Sierra Nevada and Siskiyou mountains, the desert lands on the Sunset route to New Orleans, and reached all important connections east, north, and south (even into Mexico). SP was a giant by any measure, and it had a giant fleet of steam locomotives, in a wide variety of types.

For freight, SP had hundreds of heavy "Harriman Standard" Consolidation types, it had big Mikados starting in 1911, and started with articulated locomotives in 1909 with the first ever 2-8-8-2s. Because of the snow sheds of the Sierra Nevada, SP developed the cab-forward articulated, and eventually operated almost 200 of these usual but successful locomotives. The cab-forward articulateds were the backbone of the SP heavy freight fleet from their concept in 1909 until the end of steam in the 1950s. They were, of course, oil-burners, as were many of SP's engines. In the 1920s the line even used the three-cylinder design, which was one of the alternatives proposed by some at the same time that Super Power was being developed in delivering efficient power at speed, and SP had a number of three-cylinder 4-10-2s.

In 1939 SP bought a dozen conventional 2-8-8-4s from Lima. Up to that time Lima had built only a few locomotives for SP: some switchers, Consolidations, and Mikados. These 12 locomotives were coal fired in contrast to most of SP's fleet, and they were conventionally arranged articulateds, the only such on SP at the time they arrived. The group was designated for handling heavy trains between El Paso, Texas, and Tucumcari, New Mexico. Their major dimensions were very close to the SP's cab-forward 4-8-8-2s. They also can be considered to be semi-streamlined, with a solid pilot and skyline casing. They were given Class AC-9, road numbers 3800-3811, and remained in operation until the coming of diesels, being retired between 1954 and 1956.

The sixty 4-8-4 types that Lima delivered between 1936 and 1943 were the locomotives for which the SP became famous (along with its cab-forwards). These were semi-streamlined beauties that first came for the fabulous new *Daylight* trains, and eventually handled most of SP's premier passenger fleet. Some of them (notably those built in 1943 during WWII) were designed for dual service because of War Production Board restrictions. The Classification of the first locomotives was GS (General Service, or more commonly "Golden State"). The Lima units were

SOUTHERN PACIFIC CLASS GS-2 NO. 4410-4415 ORDER NO. 1135									
DELIVERED	DECEMBER, 1936					CONSTRUCTION NUMBERS		7646-7651	
WHEEL ARRANGEMENT	DRIVING WHEEL DIAMETER		CYLINDERS		BOILER		FIREBOX		
			DIAMETER	STROKE	DIAMETER	PRESSURE	LENGTH	WIDTH	GRATE AREA
4-8-4	73½"		27"	30"	86"	250 p.s.i.	127 1/16"	102¼"	90.4 SQ.FT.
WHEEL BASE			TRACTIVE POWER		FACTOR OF ADHESION		TUBES AND FLUES		
DRIVING	ENGINE	ENGINE AND TENDER	MAIN CYLINDERS WITH BOOSTER				NUMBER	DIAMETER	LENGTH
20'	45' 10"	94' 5"	62,200 lbs. 74,100 lbs.		4.28		49 198	2¼" 3½"	21' 6"
AVERAGE WEIGHT IN WORKING ORDER, POUNDS					HEATING SURFACES, SQUARE FEET				
ON DRIVERS	TRUCK	TRAILER		TOTAL ENGINE	TUBES AND FLUES	FIREBOX & COMB. CHAM.	SYPHONS	TOTAL	SUPERHEATER
		FRONT AXLE	REAR AXLE						
266,500	77,400	46,300	58,200	448,400	4,502	350		4858	2086
TENDER									
TYPE	FUEL	WATER	WEIGHT, FULLY LOADED						
12 WHEEL	6,010 GALS OIL	22,000 GALS	372,880 LBS.						

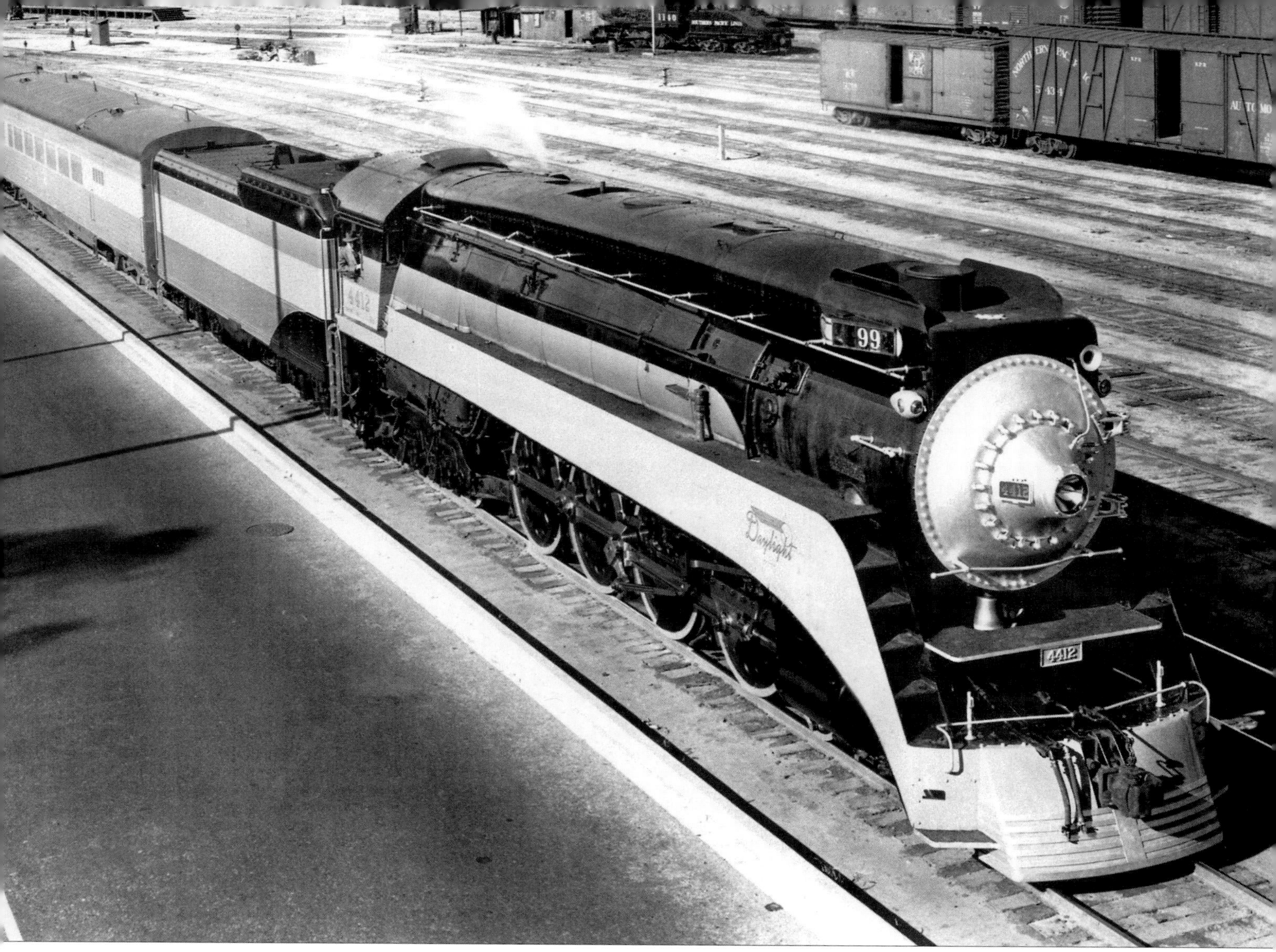
99
4412
Daylight
4412

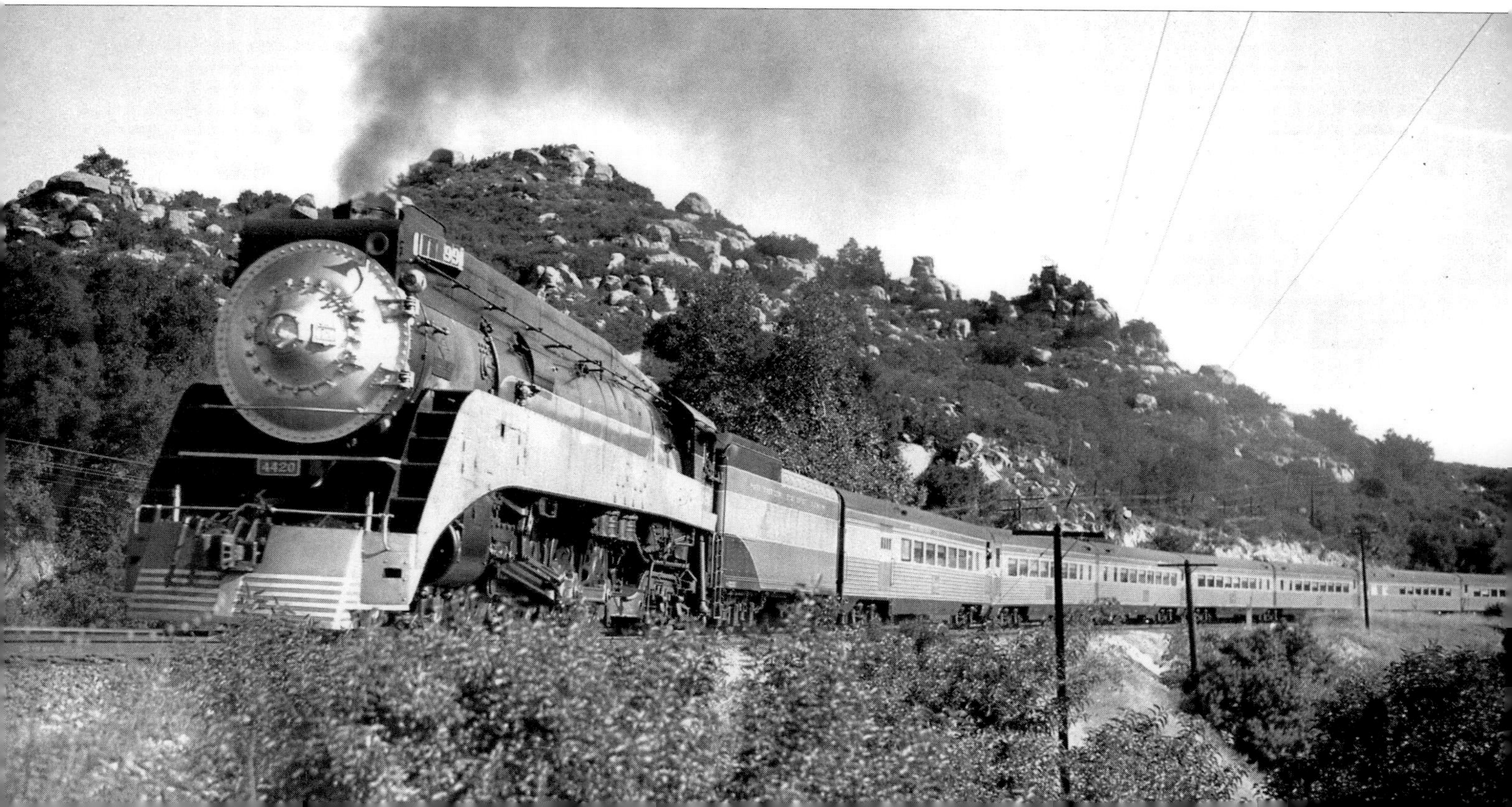
99
4420

GS-2 through GS-6. The GS-1s were the first 4-8-4s on the line, built in 1930 by Baldwin. The GS-2s were specifically ordered to power the new *Daylight* service, between San Francisco and Los Angeles, which became the most successful set of passenger trains on the SP and perhaps in America.

The GS-2s were numbered 4410-4415 and were wonderfully designed and painted. SP wanted a locomotive that would handle the new 12-car train over the 2.2 and 1 percent grades of the Coast Line at high speeds, which would cut considerable running time from previous schedules. *Railway Age* describes the appearance of the GS-2s in this way:

> Not only have these locomotives been streamlined by enclosing the sandbox, dome and other equipment mounted on the top of the boiler within a smooth casing, with the headlight enclosed within a casing which is flared into the smokebox door, but a striking color effect has also been achieved by the extensive use of red and orange on the sides of the locomotive and tender. The smokebox front is painted aluminum and the train number indicators are aluminum with black stripes. The pilot with its streamline hood is orange with aluminum bands. The name of the train is lettered in aluminum on the orange of the streamline apron which extends down from the running board on each side. The [Daylight] emblem associated with the lettering is in red outlined in black. The marker lamps are aluminum. The cylinders are finished in black, with the guides, the main and side rods and the motion work are steel with a highly polished finish. The tires and wheel rims on all wheels are painted aluminum with steps and grab handles cadmium plated. The red on the sides of the boiler above the running board and on the side of the tender, separated by the band or orange, will match the same colors on the sides of the coaches and the yellow panel will line up with the window panel of the coaches.

Opposite Above: GS-2 No. 4412 was one of the first SP streamlined 4-8-4s purchased in 1937 specifically for the new Daylights. This slightly overhead view shows how the skyline casing was arranged, and the arrangement of the smoke deflectors on each side of the stack. The train is on the inaugural run of the Coast Daylight in 1938. (Joe Schmitz Collection)

Opposite Below: GS-3 No 4420 had No. 99, the Daylight in a curve near Santa Susana, California, in 1940, with only a light wisp of oil smoke from the stack. The Daylight trains were among the biggest money-making passenger trains of all time. Note the air pumps hanging below the skirting accentuated by this side-lit view. (Joe Schmitz Collection)

As every railfan knows, the *Daylight* 4-8-4s became the darlings of the train riding public at the close of the streamline decade of the 1930s, and would become in time one of the most recognizable locomotive designs of all time. At the time SP bragged in advertisements that these were: "Unlike many recently built locomotives the two cross-compound air compressors on each of these engines are mounted on the left side of the boiler, partially concealed under the running-board. . . . The tender is of the rectangular type and is designed in cross-section to conform with the exterior of the coaches of the train." It carried 6,010 gallons of oil fuel and 22,000 gallons of water.

A second order for 14 more (GS-3) similar locomotives was received by the end of 1938, but these were somewhat heavier and had 80-inch drivers instead of the 73-½-inch wheels on the GS-2s. Boiler pressure increased by 30 pounds to 280 psi, and there was a greater length of wheel base. Some of the reciprocating parts were lightened. The boiler combustion chamber was increased 20 inches as well (for a total of 80 inches), and the boiler was of nickel steel rather than the earlier design of carbon steel.

Greatly satisfied with Lima's products, SP received 30 more in 1941-42 (GS-4 & GS-5) with a boiler pressure of 300 psi. The two GS-5s differed from their GS-4 sisters in that they were equipped with roller bearings.

Then, in 1943, ten more arrived, but dimensions changed and the streamlined skirt and paint were eliminated because of the war. They reverted to 73-½-inch drivers and were designed for dual freight/passenger service. When the SP locomotives were built (classed GS-6), only four were actually delivered to the SP, the other six were delivered to the Western Pacific. A new order was placed with Lima for six additional locomotives for SP to replace the ones that went to the WP (see page 137). Central of Georgia 4-8-4s were also built to this standard but without the skyline casing. (see page 139)

SP started dieselization in earnest in 1947 and it was completed a decade later. GS-4 No. 4449 was donated to Portland, Oregon, in 1958, and was displayed there until 1975 when it was restored to service to pull the American Freedom Train. Subsequently it hauled many excursion trains.

NOTE: There was one other class of Lima Super Power on the SP, that being ten second-hand Boston & Maine 2-8-4s which came to the line in 1945 to help with traffic late in WWII. B&M's 20 2-8-4s were all sold off, 10 to SP and 10 to AT&SF.

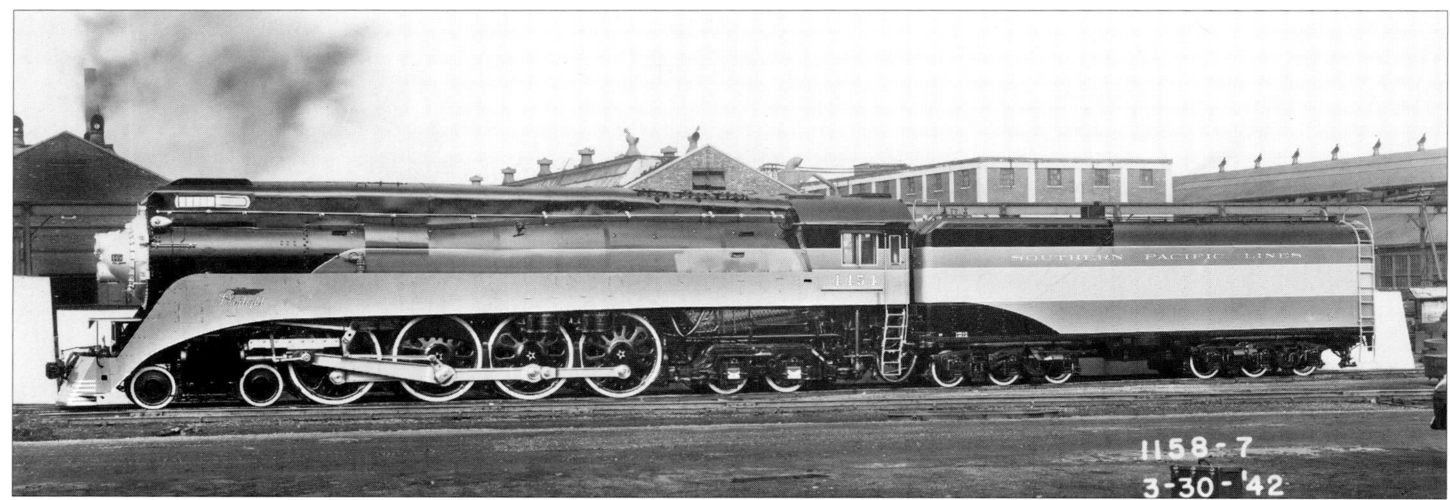

Lima builder broadside of an SP GS-4, No. 4454, March 30, 1942. Even in the monochrome photo, the striking color is evident. There is hardly a locomotive fan in the country who is not familiar with this famous class. (Lima Photo, Kevin Kohls Collection)

Leaving Los Angeles Union Station, GS-3 No. 4424 is on short Train No. 51 in about 1940. This locomotive would hardly have to breathe to propel this five-car consist. (Jay Williams Collection)

SOUTHERN PACIFIC CLASS GS-3 NO. 4416-4429 ORDER NO. 1141

DELIVERED	4416-4420: OCTOBER, 1937; 4421-4426: NOVEMBER, 1937; 4427-4429: DECEMBER, 1937					CONSTRUCTION NUMBERS		7721-7734	
WHEEL ARRANGEMENT	DRIVING WHEEL DIAMETER	CYLINDERS		BOILER		FIREBOX			
		DIAMETER	STROKE	DIAMETER	PRESSURE	LENGTH	WIDTH	GRATE AREA	
4-8-4	80"	26"	32"	86"	280 p.s.i.	127 1/16"	102¼"	90.4 SQ.FT.	
WHEEL BASE			TRACTIVE POWER	FACTOR OF ADHESION		TUBES AND FLUES			
DRIVING	ENGINE	ENGINE AND TENDER	MAIN CYLINDERS WITH BOOSTER			NUMBER	DIAMETER	LENGTH	
21' 6"	47' 8"	95' 10½"	62,800 lbs. 75,000 lbs.	4.25		49 198	2¼" 3½"	21' 6"	
AVERAGE WEIGHT IN WORKING ORDER, POUNDS					HEATING SURFACES, SQUARE FEET				
ON DRIVERS	TRUCK	TRAILER FRONT AXLE	TRAILER REAR AXLE	TOTAL ENGINE	TUBES AND FLUES	FIREBOX & COMB. CHAM.	SYPHONS	TOTAL	SUPERHEATER
267,300	83,300	49,500	59,900	460,000	4,502	385		4887	2086
TENDER									
TYPE	FUEL	WATER	WEIGHT, FULLY LOADED						
12 WHEEL	6,010 GALS OIL	22,000 GALS	372,880 LBS.						

SOUTHERN PACIFIC CLASS GS-4 NO. 4430-4449 ORDER NO. 1152
SOUTHERN PACIFIC CLASS GS-4 NO. 4450-4457 ORDER NO. 1158
SOUTHERN PACIFIC CLASS GS-5 NO. 4458-4459 ORDER NO. 1158

DELIVERED	4430-4431: MARCH, 1941; 4432:4444: APRIL, 1941; 4445-4449: MAY, 1941 4450-4454: MARCH, 1942; 4455-4456: APRIL, 1942; 4458-4459: JUNE, 1942 4457: JUNE, 1942;					CONSTRUCTION NUMBERS		Nos. 4430-4449: 7798-7817 Nos. 4450-4447: 7848-7855 Nos. 4458-4459: 7856-7857	
WHEEL ARRANGEMENT	DRIVING WHEEL DIAMETER	CYLINDERS		BOILER		FIREBOX			
		DIAMETER	STROKE	DIAMETER	PRESSURE	LENGTH	WIDTH	GRATE AREA	
4-8-4	80"	25½"	32"	86"	300 p.s.i.	127 1/8"	102¼"	90.4 SQ.FT.	
WHEEL BASE			TRACTIVE POWER	FACTOR OF ADHESION		TUBES AND FLUES			
DRIVING	ENGINE	ENGINE AND TENDER	MAIN CYLINDERS WITH BOOSTER			NUMBER	DIAMETER	LENGTH	
21' 6"	47' 8"	96' 3"	64,760 lbs. 77,760 lbs.	4.28		49 198	2¼" 3½"	21' 6"	
AVERAGE WEIGHT IN WORKING ORDER, POUNDS					HEATING SURFACES, SQUARE FEET				
ON DRIVERS	TRUCK	TRAILER FRONT AXLE	TRAILER REAR AXLE	TOTAL ENGINE	TUBES AND FLUES	FIREBOX & COMB. CHAM.	SYPHONS	TOTAL	SUPERHEATER
275,700	81,300	56,000	62,000	475,000	4,502	385		4887	2086
TENDER									
TYPE	FUEL	WATER	WEIGHT, 2/3 LOAD						
12 WHEEL	5,880 GALS OIL	23,300 GALS	313,730 LBS.						

SOUTHERN PACIFIC CLASS GS-6 NO. 4460-4463 ORDER NO. 1167
SOUTHERN PACIFIC CLASS GS-6 NO. 4464-4469 ORDER NO. 1172

DELIVERED	4460-4462: JULY, 1943; 4463: AUGUST, 1943 4464-4469: AUGUST, 1943					CONSTRUCTION NUMBERS		Nos. 4460-4463: 8013-8016 Nos. 4464-4469: 8248-8253	
WHEEL ARRANGEMENT	DRIVING WHEEL DIAMETER	CYLINDERS		BOILER		FIREBOX			
		DIAMETER	STROKE	DIAMETER	PRESSURE	LENGTH	WIDTH	GRATE AREA	
4-8-4	73½"	27"	30"	86"	260 p.s.i.	127 1/16"	102¼"	90.2 SQ.FT.	
WHEEL BASE			TRACTIVE POWER	FACTOR OF ADHESION		TUBES AND FLUES			
DRIVING	ENGINE	ENGINE AND TENDER	MAIN CYLINDERS WITH BOOSTER			NUMBER	DIAMETER	LENGTH	
20'	45' 10"	94' 5"	64,200 lbs. 75,500 lbs.	4.42		49 198	2¼" 3½"	21' 6"	
AVERAGE WEIGHT IN WORKING ORDER, POUNDS					HEATING SURFACES, SQUARE FEET				
ON DRIVERS	TRUCK	TRAILER FRONT AXLE	TRAILER REAR AXLE	TOTAL ENGINE	TUBES AND FLUES	FIREBOX & COMB. CHAM.	SYPHONS	TOTAL	SUPERHEATER
283,200	72,700	50,000	62,500	468,400	4,502	350		4852	2086
TENDER									
TYPE	FUEL	WATER	WEIGHT, 2/3 LOAD						
12 WHEEL	6,080 GALS OIL	23,200 GALS	317,800 LBS.						

GS-3 No. 4422 takes freight train No. 46 around a curve east of Sparks, Nevada, in November 1946. By this time the locomotive's Daylight colors have been overpainted and a big road name appears on the tender. These engines certainly had the power to handle fast freight as well a passenger jobs. (TLC Collection)

Another Lima photo, this time No. 4436, gives a good appreciation for the size and first impression of the type. The conical housing on the smokebox door gave it the appropriate bullet nose, but kept the door easily accessible, just as the skirting allowed complete access to the running gear. The top headlight was of the oscillating type. (Lima Photo, Kevin Kohls Collection)

No. 4458 in its head-on smokebox portrait new at Lima in 1942, shows clearly the oscillating upper headlight. On many streamlined locomotives the front coupler could be folded into the solid pilot, but on the these it could not. (Lima Photo, Kevin Kohls Collection)

This great photo shows the Lima erecting floor March 1, 1941, while five GS-4s are being built, each is at a slightly different stage of production. (Lima Photo, Kevin Kohls Collection)

No. 4457 at speed in 1954, toward the end of its service. This photo taken from a following automobile certainly gives the proper impression of speed. (Robert Hale Photo, Jay Williams Collection)

Train No 96, the Noon Daylight is passing Chittenden Pass, California, in 1948 with No. 4444 in charge, trailing a cloud of white exhaust. There could hardly be imagined a more beautiful train. (Joe Schmitz Collection)

GS-4 No. 4459 is seen at speed with one of the Daylights (No. 98) at Gerber, California, April 29, 1951. These locomotives had no trouble keeping a fast schedule with heavy trains such as this (17 cars in this case). (TLC Collection)

Radial tracks at SP's passenger roundhouse in San Francisco in 1952 are populated with a variety of Lima 4-8-4s. (Joe Schmitz Collection)

The GS-6 class came in 1943 and was quite different from the preceding locomotive of the type, shorn of its bright colors and skirting, it has a very utilitarian look. Because of War Production Board limitations the class had to be built for dual purpose freight and passenger work, and came with 73-½ inch drivers. (Lima Photo, Kevin Kohls Collection)

GS-6 No. 4463 ready to take a freight at San Jose, California, January 1953. By this late date the road name on the tender has been changed to the large letters. (R. C. Gray Photo, TLC Collection)

SOUTHERN PACIFIC CLASS AC-9 NO. 3800-3811 ORDER NO. 1148									
DELIVERED	3800-3809: OCTOBER, 1939; 3810-3812: NOVEMBER, 1939					CONSTRUCTION NUMBERS		7765-7776	
WHEEL ARRANGEMENT	DRIVING WHEEL DIAMETER	CYLINDERS		BOILER		FIREBOX			
		DIAMETER	STROKE	DIAMETER	PRESSURE	LENGTH	WIDTH	GRATE AREA	
2-8-8-4	63½"	24"	32"	109 1/8"	250 p.s.i.	205 21/32"	102¼"	139.3 SQ.FT.	
WHEEL BASE			TRACTIVE POWER		FACTOR OF ADHESION		TUBES AND FLUES		
DRIVING	ENGINE	ENGINE AND TENDER	MAIN CYLINDERS				NUMBER	DIAMETER	LENGTH
44' 7"	66' 3"	112' 11 7/8"	124,300 lbs.		4.27		86 260	2¼" 3½"	22'
AVERAGE WEIGHT IN WORKING ORDER, POUNDS					HEATING SURFACES, SQUARE FEET				
ON DRIVERS	TRUCK	TRAILER		TOTAL ENGINE	TUBES AND FLUES	FIREBOX & COMB. CHAM.	CIRCULATORS	TOTAL	SUPERHEATER
		FRONT AXLE	REAR AXLE						
531,200	48,300	48,900	61,500	689,900	6,329	465	124	6,918	2,831
TENDER									
TYPE	FUEL	WATER	WEIGHT, FULLY LOADED						
12 WHEEL	28 TONS	22,120 GALS	400,700 LBS.						

Another classic Lima builder photo of No. 3800, the first of the AC-9 class shining brilliantly for its portrait. It has a flying pumps front end with rectangular smokebox and pilot-mounted headlight similar to C&O's H-8 2-6-6-6s that would come along in a couple of years from Lima. A characteristic SP air horn hides to the upper left. (Lima Photo, Kevin Kohls Collection)

GS-6's were well at home on passenger runs as as well, as attested by this photo. (Jay Williams Collection)

This Lima broadside of the AC-9 reveals a powerful locomotive, made all the more compact looking with its skyline casing. This is as close as an articulated ever came to being streamlined! (Lima Photo, Kevin Kohls Collection)

Left side of No. 3800 at Kansas City, as it is being delivered new from Lima to SP, Nov. 1, 1939. The Lima advertising sign is attached to the handrail. (Jay Williams Collection)

Well-worn AC-9 No. 3805 at El Paso, Texas, May 15, 1951. These dozen locomotives were purchased strictly for the El Paso-Tucumcari run. (Jay Williams Collection)

The Kansas City Southern operated a main line that ran almost directly north-south between Kansas City, Missouri, and Port Arthur, Texas. The road was built to provide a fast straight line between the Midwest and Port Arthur to meet shipping in the Gulf of Mexico. The Texas oil boom contributed importantly to its traffic both in the oil itself and the attendant economic activity that it engendered.

KCS had a roster of relatively small locomotives, including 2-8-0s, 2-10-2s, and 2-8-8-0 articulateds. The road's most adverse sections were were in the Ozarks in southwest Missouri and along the Oklahoma-Arkansas border. The Mallets and 2-10-2s were heavily used in this region.

The road jumped into the Super Power era in 1937 when it ordered ten 2-10-4 Texas types from Lima, which were given Class J and road numbers 900-909. They would by the last 2-10-4s that Lima built, and were the last new steam locomotives that KCS bought.

These were great looking locomotives, with all the attributes of Super Power, including a large grate area of 107 square feet. One remarkable feature was a boiler pressure of 310 psi, the highest that had been used in stay bolt type fireboxes up to that time.

Large boilers of 92 inches in the first course and 102 inches at the third course were made of nickel steel. Nos. 905-909 were fired with coal and Nos. 900-904 with oil, since the latter fuel was readily available on the KCS line. They had Worthington Type 6SA feedwater heaters in the smokebox and a Type E superheater, with 3-3/4 inch tubes, which *Railway Age* reported as among the first uses of this size. They had a General Steel Castings cast bed with cylinders cast integral. Drivers and engine truck wheels were fitted with SKF roller bearings. The trailing truck was fitted with friction bearings, but with provision for later replacement with roller bearings.

Railway Age made an uncharacteristic remark about the appearance of the locomotives: "These locomotives present an exceptionally neat appearance. Not only does this apply to the exterior of the locomotives, but also to the back heads within the cab as well."

Two sand boxes were used, just in front of and behind the steam dome, but both still well forward on the boiler top.

The new 2-10-4s went to work replacing some of the Mallets as well as the 2-10-2s, and were especially used in the territory between Kansas City and De Queen, Arkansas. A contemporary comment on their service: ". . . . [They] have given excellent performance from the standpoint of meeting the fast schedules with good train load and, at the same time, producing economy in fuel consumption as well as in maintenance."

KANSAS CITY SOUTHERN CLASS J NO. 900-909 ORDER NO. 1138										
DELIVERED		900-904: JULY, 1937; 905-908: AUGUST, 1937; 909: SEPTEMBER, 1937					CONSTRUCTION NUMBERS		7660-7669	
WHEEL ARRANGEMENT		DRIVING WHEEL DIAMETER		CYLINDERS		BOILER		FIREBOX		
2-10-4		70"		DIAMETER	STROKE	DIAMETER	PRESSURE	LENGTH	WIDTH	GRATE AREA
				27"	34"	92"	310 p.s.i.	150"	102 1/8"	107 SQ.FT.
WHEEL BASE				TRACTIVE POWER		FACTOR OF ADHESION		TUBES AND FLUES		
DRIVING	ENGINE		ENGINE AND TENDER	MAIN CYLINDERS				NUMBER	DIAMETER	LENGTH
24' 4"	48' 8"		98' 5"	93,300 lbs.		3.75		73 183	2¼" 3¾"	21' 0"
AVERAGE WEIGHT IN WORKING ORDER, POUNDS						HEATING SURFACES, SQUARE FEET				
ON DRIVERS 900-904 905-909	TRUCK		TRAILER FRONT AXLE	TRAILER REAR AXLE	TOTAL ENGINE	TUBES AND FLUES	FIREBOX & COMB. CHAM.	SYPHONS	TOTAL	SUPERHEATER
350,000 353,300	50,600 51,500		53,200 53,600	55,200 55,600	509,000 514,000	4,654	446	54	5,154	2,075
TENDER										
TYPE	FUEL		WATER	WEIGHT, FULLY LOADED						
12 WHEEL	4,500 GALS OIL 24 TONS		21,000 GALS 20,700 GALS	348,000 LBS.						

Lima builder's photo of KCS #900 (Lima photo, Allen County Hist. Soc. Collection)

Pulling out of Kansas City on November 20, 1949, oil-fired class J No. 900 is well maintained and exudes the power one expects of a Texas type. The size and power of the big 2-10-4 is still well illustrated in this photo, where the clean lines of boiler topped by the giant casing with the sandbox and steam dome are evident. The traditional clean Super Power front with centered headlight and shielded pumps with the high bell make these a truly excellent example of the last of the Lima Texas types. (Jay Williams Collection)

No. 905 at Kansas City on March 16, 1947 shows all the clean boiler lines with which it was built, causing Railway Age to comment on its clean and pleasing appearance. The Boxpok drivers always seem to lend an air of power to a locomotive. The Lima builder plate had a large "J" cast into it, the only Lima plate ever to carry the railroad class for a locomotive. Note also the enclosed cab. (Jay Williams Collection)

Wisconsin Central (Soo Line)

The Minneapolis, St. Paul & Sault Ste. Marie Railway (known as the Soo Line since "Sault" is pronounced "Soo") operated in the upper Midwestern U. S., mainly hauling wheat and other grains to market. It operated numerous lines in North Dakota, Minnesota, Wisconsin, and Iowa with mainline connections to Chicago. The Twin Cities of Minneapolis & St. Paul were a hub of its lines and activities. Not a strong company financially, it suffered considerably during the Depression and went to bankruptcy in 1937 (emerging in 1944). The Soo Line of today is part of Canadian National. Part of its main lines were operated as a separate corporation under the name Wisconsin Central, whose equipment was lettered separately from the main company's. The Wisconsin Central's main line was between Chicago and Minneapolis, and was largely a single track which was longer than other routes between these points.

Soo's motive power fleet boasted a variety of types with Consolidations and Mikados as the main stays for freight service. Since it had no topographical challenges, heavy power wasn't really needed.

Because it suffered from an inferior position on the important Twin Cities-Chicago market, about the only thing it could do to really compete was to offer better service and achieve higher speeds in order to offset the greater length of its route. With much of its line as single track it had to be able to operate on a high level of efficiency in order to keep the line open and running.

Even though it was in bankruptcy, the line was allowed to order four 4-8-4 types from Lima in 1938 (on the account of subsidiary Wisconsin Central). These would be the only Lima-built locomotives the railway ever owned and were the last steam it ever bought. With the 4-8-4 wheel arrangement and 75-inch drivers, locomotives such as these could have been expected to be used in passenger service, but Soo had very little important passenger trains and none needed such heavy power. Besides, it had been using the 4-8-2 Mountain types, also usually passenger power, for

Opposite Top: Lima builders view of O-20 Class No. 5000. Tiny sub-lettering "W. C." under the number on the cab indicates that this is Wisconsin Central equipment, though the Soo line emblem adorns the tender side. A solid, powerful looking, compact locomotive in the Super Power mold, with Boxpox drivers. The tender seems bit short for this type of locomotive, but still rode on six-wheel trucks. This was to accommodate turntable lengths. (Lima Photo, Kevin Kohls Collection)

Opposite Center: No. 5001 is impressive from this angle as it awaits assignments at Minneapolis on August 24, 1941. The clean face, shielded pumps, clean boiler, spacious cab, Boxpok drivers, all contribute to this look. The headlight is mounted a little higher than usual, and the sand pipes are encased. The slightly off center headlight was a Soo characteristic. (Jay Williams Collection)

Opposite Bottom: Right side view of 5003 taken at Minneapolis on Sept. 26, 1946, with one oddity being the spoked engine truck wheel, probably a replacement. (Jay Williams Collection)

SOO LINE CLASS O-20 NO. 5000-5003 ORDER NO. 1145

DELIVERED	5000-5003: JANUARY, 1938	CONSTRUCTION NUMBERS	7753-7756

WHEEL ARRANGEMENT	DRIVING WHEEL DIAMETER	CYLINDERS		BOILER		FIREBOX		
		DIAMETER	STROKE	DIAMETER	PRESSURE	LENGTH	WIDTH	GRATE AREA
4-8-4	75"	26"	32"	86"	270 p.s.i.	132 ⅛"	96¼"	88.3 SQ.FT.

WHEEL BASE			TRACTIVE POWER	FACTOR OF ADHESION		TUBES AND FLUES		
DRIVING	ENGINE	ENGINE AND TENDER	MAIN CYLINDERS			NUMBER	DIAMETER	LENGTH
19' 9"	46' 9"	87' 9½"	66,000 lbs.	3.99		65 199	2¼" 3½"	21' 6"

AVERAGE WEIGHT IN WORKING ORDER, POUNDS					HEATING SURFACES, SQUARE FEET				
ON DRIVERS	TRUCK	TRAILER FRONT AXLE	TRAILER REAR AXLE	TOTAL ENGINE	TUBES AND FLUES	FIREBOX & COMB. CHAM.	SYPHONS	TOTAL	SUPERHEATER
263,000	76,000	52,300	54,200	445,500	4,719	376	47	5,142	2,120

TENDER			
TYPE	FUEL	WATER	*WEIGHT, ⅔ LOAD*
12 WHEEL	24 TONS	17,500 GALS	252,967 LBS.

5000
5000

5001
5001
5001

5003
5003

its fast freight traffic. The 4-8-4s were given O-20 class and assigned road numbers 5000-5003.

Just four 4-8-4s would seem to be a small number, and indeed they it was. They were intended for a very specific service: handling the Soo's fastest freight trains on the Wisconsin Central main line between Chicago and the Twin Cities. They were a class above everything else on the railroad. The new locomotives covered the line's four most important trains, Nos. 24 and 26 from Shoreham yard in Minneapolis to Schiller Park yard in Chicago and Nos. 23 and 25 in the westbound direction.

The scheduled terminal-to-terminal time for these trains was 18 hours and 40 minutes eastbound and 16 hours and 50 minutes westbound (that amounted to actual running time of 16 hours 20 minutes eastbound and 14 hours and 55 minutes westbound when allowance for stopped time at terminals was deducted). Reported actual running times using the new Lima 4-8-4s was often less than this, and the railroad was extremely pleased with the performance.

The second most important aspect of the O-20 class 4-8-4s was their reliability and availability. During their first full year of operation they ran up a total of 100,000 miles with little shop time. This resulted in an increase in train speed and gross ton miles per hour of up to 30%. Engineers recalled (in Cook's *Lima Super Power* book) that they had speed recorders and were often able to get trains of between 3,000 and 4,000 tons going at 70 mph, but required a couple of switchers helping to get them out of yards, because those high drivers were made for running, not for starting.

Soo line dieselized, along with all the other railroads, in the late 1940s and early 1950s. F3s bumped the O's to the sidetrack by 1954. Although not well remembered because of the small number of units involved on a railroad that doesn't get all that much press, they served a particular need at a particular time and place uncommonly well.

The *Railway Age* article describing these locomotives says "The design, conservative as to details, presents well-balanced proportions." They had General Steel Castings (GSC) beds with integral cylinders and back cylinder heads, main air reservoir, air-compressor supports, guide yoke, and reverse-gear bracket. The GSC engine truck had inside bearings and SCF roller-bearing wheels.

General arrangement drawing showing Soo Line 4-8-4s of O-20 class (From Locomotive Cyclopedia)

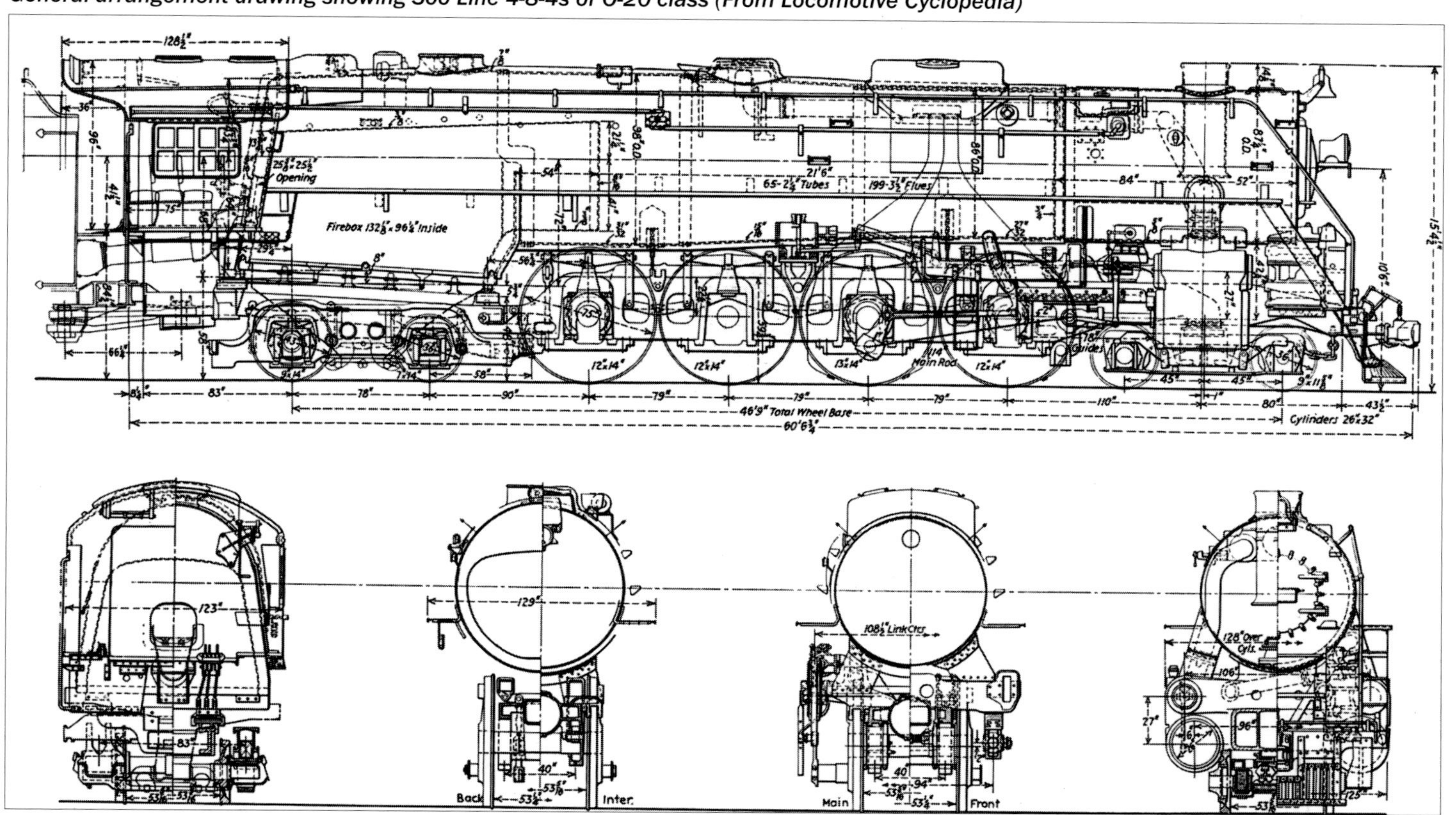

Grand Trunk Western

The Grand Trunk Western Railway was the U. S. subsidiary of Canadian National Railway, operating a main line from Port Huron, Michigan, to Chicago, so as to reach the great railroad hub. It was an integral part of the Canadian National system, but had the separate operational and corporate existence for its U. S. lines.

Of course, CN had a huge locomotive fleet. Some of its locomotives were built in the U. S. and others in Canada. For its passenger trains, CN had just over 200 of the 4-8-4 type built between 1927 and 1944, which it used in dual service for both passenger and freight trains. This was the largest fleet of 4-8-4s anywhere, ever. Of this huge fleet Lima built six 4-8-4s in 1938, which had GTW road numbers 6405-6409 and Class U-4b (meshing with the main CN fleet numbering). GTW also had 37 Alco 4-8-4 engines built in 1927 and in 1942. Along with a considerable stable of 4-8-2 types built in the same era, these were the largest and most powerful locomotives on CN lines.

The six Lima engines were given a semi-streamlining that was first developed by the National Research Council in Ottawa, for CN's own U-4a class, built by Montreal Locomotive Works the year before. The grill vents ahead of the stack served as a smoke lifter to throw the smoke high above the cab. Unlike most other Lima-built Super Power locomotives, they had Vanderbilt tenders.

These 4-8-4s were designated to handle the GTW's passenger trains the 334 miles between Port Huron and Chicago. They ran an average of about 10,000 miles per month with trains ranging up to 15 cars in length. They had an outstanding maintenance record and, as an example, averaged 200,000 miles per locomotive before they had to have driving tires replaced.

Lima builder broadside shows the streamlining used on the GTW 4-8-4s which could be considered to be a semi-streamlining since the tender isn't covered with a cowl and the boiler simply has a clean exterior and a skyline casing. (Lima Photo, Kevin Kohls Collection)

GRAND TRUNK WESTERN CLASS U-4B NO. 6405-6409 ORDER NO. 1147									
DELIVERED	6405-6406: JULY, 1938; 6407-6409: AUGUST, 1938					CONSTRUCTION NUMBERS		7759-7764	
WHEEL ARRANGEMENT	DRIVING WHEEL DIAMETER		CYLINDERS		BOILER		FIREBOX		
			DIAMETER	STROKE	DIAMETER	PRESSURE	LENGTH	WIDTH	GRATE AREA
4-8-4	77"		24"	30"	79 9/16"	275 p.s.i.	126 1/8"	84 3/16"	73.7 SQ.FT.
WHEEL BASE			TRACTIVE POWER		FACTOR OF ADHESION		TUBES AND FLUES		
DRIVING	ENGINE	ENGINE AND TENDER	MAIN CYLINDERS				NUMBER	DIAMETER	LENGTH
20'	44' 1½"	82' 8¼"	52,500 lbs.		4.53		43 146	2¼" 3½"	21' 10"
AVERAGE WEIGHT IN WORKING ORDER, POUNDS					HEATING SURFACES, SQUARE FEET				
ON DRIVERS	TRUCK	TRAILER		TOTAL ENGINE	TUBES AND FLUES	FIREBOX & COMB. CHAM.	SYPHONS	TOTAL	SUPERHEATER
		FRONT AXLE	REAR AXLE						
237,900	62,000	37,700	45,100	382,700	3,458	296	98	3,852	1,530
TENDER									
TYPE	FUEL	WATER	WEIGHT, FULLY LOADED						
12 WHEEL	20 TONS	14,300 GALS	278,500 LBS.						

There were four through trains between Toronto and Chicago via the Grand Trunk from Port Huron, east and westbound sections of the *International Limited* and the *Maple Leaf*.

The big streamlined 4-8-4s had a grand appearance with green tenders, cab and running board, gun-metal boiler, and black smokebox and front end. The GTW herald and road number on the running board were gold with a red background, and pin striping was in gold. The drivers were Boxpok type. The tender had six-wheel trucks placed fairly close together since it was shorter than most tenders for this type of engine with its 14,300 gallons of water capacity.

The Grand Trunk was late in dieselizing its passenger trains and the U-4b class ran until the fall of 1959.

No. 6408 was ten years old when it was used as part of GTWs display at the 1949 Chicago Railroad Fair. At that time it was the newest and fanciest thing on the line. (TLC Collection)

At Chicago between runs on June 11, 1948, No. 6408 is shining clean, right down to the white tires on its wheels. The streamlining was duplicative to CN's, which was designed by the National Research Council in Ottawa, and first employed on CN's 4-8-4s in 1936. The Lima engines of 1938 were duplicates. The enclosed cab was standard for many CN locomotives. (Jay Williams Collection)

The Western Pacific operated lines in northern California, crossing the famed Sierra Nevada Mountains into northern Nevada and across Utah to Salt Lake City. Its crossing of the mountains was at an altitude lower than Southern Pacific's, which helped offset the fact that its route was a good deal longer. The WP was a latecomer to the railroad picture in California, not being created until 1903. It was essentially a mainline with few branches, and none of any consequence, so it had to rely very much on traffic originating on other lines. Through financial alliances it was able to secure a lucrative north-south haul through California to augment the advantages of its east-west routing across California, Nevada, and Utah. Connection with the Denver & Rio Grande Western was both financial and physical.

In its formative years WP handled its freight business with 2-8-0s and 2-8-2s, and acquired 2-6-6-2s in 1917 and 1924, and 2-8-8-2s in the 1930s to challenge the mountain grades with the heaviest possible trains. Seven Alco 4-6-6-4 Challengers arrived in 1938. For passenger trains three dozen 4-6-0s were standard. Then second hand (from Florida East Coast) 4-8-2s in 1924 became the second generation of passenger steam on the

Superb Lima ¾ builder's view of WP 4-8-4 No. 485 shows its marked similarity to the SP 4-8-4s that were being built at Lima at the same time. The bullet nose and skyline casing make it different from other WP locomotives. The big oil tender on the six-wheel trucks held a huge 6,000 gallons of fuel and 23,300 gallons of water, giving the new power considerable range. It was a clean, semi-streamlined locomotive of the first order in appearance. Note the small smoke deflectors on each side of the stack. The SP's characteristic air horn is visible at front as well. (Lima Photo, Kevin Kohls Collection)

WESTERN PACIFIC CLASS GS-64-77 NO. 481-486 ORDER NO. 1167										
DELIVERED		481-482: JUNE, 1943; 483-486: JULY, 1943					CONSTRUCTION NUMBERS		8017-8022	
WHEEL ARRANGEMENT		DRIVING WHEEL DIAMETER		CYLINDERS		BOILER		FIREBOX		
				DIAMETER	STROKE	DIAMETER	PRESSURE	LENGTH	WIDTH	GRATE AREA
4-8-4		73½"		27"	30"	86"	260 p.s.i.	127 $^{1}/_{16}$"	102¼"	90.2 SQ.FT.
WHEEL BASE				TRACTIVE POWER		FACTOR OF ADHESION		TUBES AND FLUES		
DRIVING	ENGINE		ENGINE AND TENDER	MAIN CYLINDERS WITH BOOSTER				NUMBER	DIAMETER	LENGTH
20'	45' 10"		94' 5"	64,200 lbs. 75,500 lbs.		4.38		49 198	2¼" 3½"	21' 6"
AVERAGE WEIGHT IN WORKING ORDER, POUNDS						HEATING SURFACES, SQUARE FEET				
ON DRIVERS	TRUCK		TRAILER		TOTAL ENGINE	TUBES AND FLUES	FIREBOX & COMB. CHAM.	SYPHONS	TOTAL	SUPERHEATER
			FRONT AXLE	REAR AXLE						
280,950	73,650		49,500	62,000	466,100	4,502	350	70	4,922	2,086
TENDER										
TYPE	FUEL		WATER	WEIGHT, $^{2}/_{3}$ LOADED						
12 WHEEL	6,000 GALS OIL		23,300 GALS	316,250 LBS.						

WP.

WP tried diesels even before World War II, and in 1941 acquired its first EMD FT units. In 1942-43 the railroad needed more power for its heaviest passenger trains and wanted 4-8-4s similar to those delivered by Lima to C&O in 1942, but couldn't accommodate that design's axle loads. It settled for a single order from Lima for six smaller 4-8-4s that were virtual duplicates to the Southern Pacific's GS-6 class, and were in fact just built as an add-on to the SP order (see page 121). This expediency was because it ensured the quickest delivery and was approved by the industry-controlling War Production Board. This accounts for their looks. The 4-8-4 wheel arrangement with 73-inch drivers could certainly serve as a dual-purpose locomotive as well, so the choice was a good one to handle the heavy wartime passenger traffic as well as to be available after the war for dual service.

They had the SP design of the bullet nose and skyline casing and if one were to look at them without markings it would surely be assumed at first glance that they were SP locomotives, although the lacked the running board skirting. Eventually, after the war, their appearance would change as WP added smoke deflectors.

After the war, WP went back into the diesel market that it had sampled before the war, and F3 and F7 classes came along 1947 to 1950, including FP7 units for passenger trains, which included a portion of the famous *California Zephyr's* route. By 1950 the Lima 4-8-4s were largely out of a job, and in 1953 three of them were sold to SP so that they could be cannibalized for parts to keep the latter's aging fleet in service as it reached its last days as well.

The 4-8-4s, which were given WP Class GS-64-77 and road numbers 481-486, were the last new steam on the WP, and the only WP steam ever built by Lima.

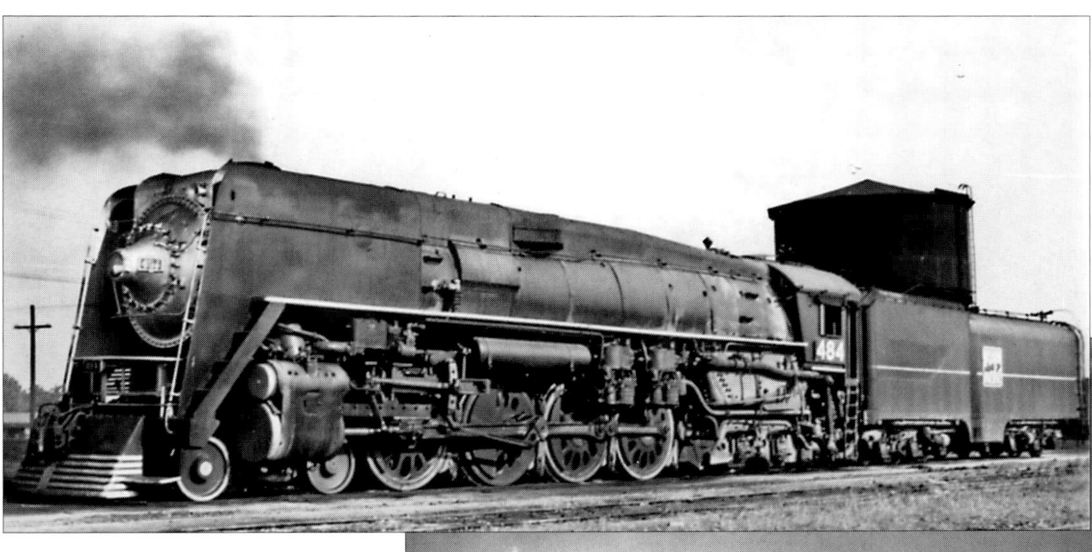

The left side is seen in this portrait view of No. 484. Note the air pumps mounted below the running board on this side, instead up front on the pilot deck as on many Lima Super Power designs. (TLC Collection)

Slightly blurred, No. 483 is coming to a fast stop at Wendover, Utah, down off a ten-mile grade with the mail/express/coach train No. 2 at 4:15 pm. (Rail Photo Service, TLC Collection)

Central of Georgia

The Central of Georgia operated lines in Georgia and Alabama and served such cities at Montgomery and Birmingham in Alabama and Columbus, Macon, Atlanta, and Savannah in Georgia. It also had a northern line that reached Chattanooga, Tennessee. Through connections, CofG served as an important bridge line for through passenger and freight trains between the Midwest and Florida. It went into receivership in 1932 and didn't emerge until 1948.

CofG's motive power consisted largely of 2-8-0s and 2-8-2s, most built before WWI. Many of the Mikados were built by Lima, with Baldwin building the remaining. Some 2-10-2s came in 1926 and ten 2-6-6-2s were built by Alco in 1919 (only to be sold to IC in 1926). For passenger locomotives the line started with Ten-wheelers, moved to Pacifics, some of which came from Lima, and ended with Mountain types in early 1920s. In 1943, at the height of war-time traffic CofG needed something in addition to the 4-8-2s on the heavy regular Midwest-Florida passenger trains that traversed its line and very heavy troop movements to and from Ft. Benning at Columbus, Georgia, and goods headed to ports on the east coast.

To alleviate the problem, CofG ordered eight 4-8-4s from Lima that were very close in major dimensions to the contemporary Southern Pacific GS-6 class "Daylight" 4-8-4s (minus the fancy bullet nose and skyline casing). They were given Class K and road numbers of 451-458. They were the only Lima Super Power on CofG and were also the very last steam built for the road. The 4-8-4s could be used, if needed, for fast freight trains as well as their intended passenger duties, and were primarily for use on the heavy grades over the southern Appalachians on the Macon and Columbus divisions.

Initially they averaged less than 100 pounds of coal per 1,000 gross ton-miles in freight service, and an average of 11.4 pounds per passenger train car-mile, according to *Railway Mechanical Engineer*. The drivers were Boxpok type of 66-inch centers and of 73-½ inch diameter with tires. The boiler was conical with 86-inch diameter at the front and 96 at the throat. Welded construction was used throughout the firebox.

The tenders were very small for a locomotive of this size and power, with 21 tons of coal capacity but holding only 13,000 gallons of water. The reason for the short tender was to accommodate turntable lengths.

These 4-8-4s put in a superb performance, but CofG bought E7s and E8s between 1946 and 1950, ending their usefulness in passenger service, and other road freight and road switcher diesels began to handle the freight, so they were all retired by 1953, after less than a decade of use.

CENTRAL OF GEORGIA CLASS K NO. 451-458 ORDER NO. 1174									
DELIVERED		451: AUGUST, 1943; 452-456: SEPTEMBER, 1943; 457-458: OCTOBER, 1943				CONSTRUCTION NUMBERS		8254-8261	
WHEEL ARRANGEMENT		DRIVING WHEEL DIAMETER	CYLINDERS		BOILER		FIREBOX		
			DIAMETER	STROKE	DIAMETER	PRESSURE	LENGTH	WIDTH	GRATE AREA
4-8-4		73½"	27"	30"	86"	250 p.s.i.	127 1/16"	102¼"	90.2 SQ.FT.
WHEEL BASE			TRACTIVE POWER		FACTOR OF ADHESION		TUBES AND FLUES		
DRIVING	ENGINE	ENGINE AND TENDER	MAIN CYLINDERS				NUMBER	DIAMETER	LENGTH
20'	45' 10"	83' 6"	63,200 lbs.		4.11		56 159	2¼" 4"	21' 6"
AVERAGE WEIGHT IN WORKING ORDER, POUNDS					HEATING SURFACES, SQUARE FEET				
ON DRIVERS	TRUCK	TRAILER		TOTAL ENGINE	TUBES AND FLUES	FIREBOX & COMB. CHAM.	SYPHONS	TOTAL	SUPERHEATER
		FRONT AXLE	REAR AXLE						
260,000	78,900	54,200	54,100	447,200	4,270	350	85	4,705	2,059
TENDER									
TYPE	FUEL	WATER	WEIGHT, 2/3 LOADED						
8 WHEEL	21 TONS	13,000 GALS	196,500 LBS.						

Left side, engine only, of CofG No. 451, first of the new batch of 4-8-4s built by Lima in 1943. The engine is shining brilliantly and has a Lima sign attached to the hand rail. Note the close placement of the trailer wheels, and the superheater installation ahead of the stack. Lima often took detailed photos of each class of locomotive that it built in addition to the often-published builder broadsides. (Lima Photo, Kevin Kohls Collection)

Tender-only Lima photo shows the short tender riding on four-wheel trucks, very unusual for a big Super Power locomotive like the K Class. (Lima Photo, Kevin Kohls Collection)

A third Lima photo, taken as the class came off the erecting floor, this time showing the rear of the tender of No. 455. Note the coal pusher ram sticking up very prominently on in this photo and the previous one. (Lima Photo, Kevin Kohls Collection)

No. 453 is pulling CofG Train No. 9, The Seminole, *southbound loaded with a lot of head-end traffic and heavyweight passenger cars near Weems, Alabama (just out of Birmingham) August 1, 1948.* The Seminole *was a Chicago-Sarasota and Miami train handled by the IC, CofG, ACL, and FEC. (R. D. Sharples Photo, Jay Williams Collection).*

Handling freight was another of the K class's jobs and here a manifest freight is in tow at Macon, Georgia, on May 3, 1948. Although 4-8-4s were generally considered passenger locomotives, several railroads used them regularly in freight service. CofG did more of this after the war-time passenger glut abated. (Jay Williams Collection)

Bibliography and References

Selected references pertaining to the background and historical development of the Lima Super Power locomotives and the railroads on which they operated. These works were consulted in the preparation of this book.

Books:

Brendel, Glenn, & York, Wayne, *765 - Official Souvenir Booklet*, Ft. Wayne Railroad Historical Society, Ft. Wayne, Ind. , 1980.

Bruce, Alfred W., *The Steam Locomotive in America*, W. W. Norton, New York, 1952.

Bryant, Keith J., Jr., Ed.; *Railroads in the Age of Regulation, 1900-1980,* Facts on File Publications, New York, 1988.

Castner, Charles B., Ronald Flanary, Patrick Dorin, *Louisville & Nashville, The Old Reliable*, TLC Publishing, Lynchburg, Va. 1996.

Cook, Richard J., *Super Power Steam Locomotives*, Golden West Books, San Marino, Ca., 1966.

Davies, Harold, North *American Steam Locomotive Builders and Their Insignia*, TLC Publishing, Inc., Forest, Va., 2005

Dixon, Thomas W., *The Texas in Ohio*, C&O Historical Society, C. Forge, Va., 2003.

Dixon, Thomas W., eidtor, *The Van Sweringen Railroad Empire*, C&O Historical Society, C. Forge, Va., 2006.

Dunscomb, Guy L., *A Century of Southern Pacific Steam Locomotives*, Dunscomb, Modesto, Calif., 1963.

Griffin, William E., *Richmond, Fredericksburg & Potomac, The Capital Cities Route*, TLC Publishing, Lynchburg, Va., 1994.

Hampton, Taylor, *Nickel Plate Road*, World Publihsing, Cleveland, 1947.

Hirsimaki, Eric, *Lima - the History*, Hundman Publishing, Edmonds, Wash., 1986.

Holland, Kevin J., *The Steam Liners*, TLC Publishing, Lynchburg, Va. 2002

__, *Berkshires of the Nickel Plate Road*, TLC Publishing, Lynchburg, Va. , 1998.

Huddleston, E. L., *Chesapeake & Ohio Super Power Stream Locomotives*, C&O Hist. Society, Clifton Forge, Va. , 2005.

__, *The Van Sweringen Berkshires*, NJ International, Hicksville, N. Y., 1986.

Huddleston, Eugene L., and Dioxn, T. W., *The Allegheny, Lima's Finest*, Hundman Publishing, Edmonds, Wash. 1984.

Johnson, Ralph P., *The Stream Locomotive in America*, Simmons-Boardman, NY, 1942.

Lewis, Lloyd D., *Virginian Railway Locomotives*, TLC Publishing, Lynchburg, Va., 1993.

Rehor, John S. *The Nickel Plate Story*, Kalmbach Publications, Milwaukee, 1967.

Shuster, Huddleston, Staufer, *C&O Power*, Staufer Publications, Medina, Ohio, 1966.

Stegner, Lloyd E., *North American Hudsons*, South Platte Press, David Nebr., 1987.

Swengel, F. M., *The American Steam Locomotive, Vol. 1, Evolution of the Steam Locomotive*, Davenport, Ia., 1967.

Trostel, Scott D., *The Detroit, Toledo & Ironton Railroad*, Cam-Tech Publishing, Fletcher, Ohio, 1988.

Wayner, Robert J., *Diesel Locomotive Rosters*, Brooklyn, N. Y.

Westing, Frederick & Alvin Staufer, *Erie Power*, Staufer Publications, Medina, Ohio, 1970.

Weitzman, David, *Superpower*, Godine, Boston, 1987.

Lima Loco Woks, *Lima Super-Power Steam Locomotives*, Lima, Ohio, 1947.

Locomotive Cyclopedia, Simmons-Boardman Pub. New York, 1930, 1941, 1947, 1950-52.

Periodicals:

Railway Age, Vol. 78, No. 4, Jan. 24, 1925, "Demand for Increased Horsepower," by W. E. Woodard.

__, Vol. 79, No. 11, Sept. 12, 1925 "Tests of 2-8-4 Locomotive on B. & A."

__, Vol. 79, No. 25, Dec. 19, 1925, "First Texas Type Locomotives for Texas & Pacific."

__, Vol. 82, No. 28, July 11, 1927 "Relation of Locomotive Development to Cost of Operation," by W. H. Winterrowd, VP, Lima Locomotive Works.

__, Vol. 83, No. 15, Oct. 8, 1927, "Erie Acquires 2-8-4 Locomotives for Freight Service."

__, Vol. 83, No. 17, Oct. 22, 1927, "Erie Places 2-8-4 Type Locomotives in Freight Service."

__, Vol. 84, No. 20, May 18, 1928, "The Locomotive as a Factor in Fuel Economy," by A. W. Bruce, Designing Engineer, American Locomotive Co.

__, Vol. 86, No. 15, April 20, 1929, "Modern Locomotives for Secondary Service," by W. E. Woodard, VP, Lima Locomotive Works.

__,Vol. 90, No. 5, Jan. 31, 1931, "Characteristics of Modern Locomotives."

__, Vol. 102, No. 8, Feb. 20, 1937, "Largest Streamline Steam Locomotives."

__, Vol. 104, No. 26, _____,1938, "High-Capacity Passenger Power for Southern Pacific."

__, Vol. 105, No. 14, Oct. 1, 1938, "Soo Line Locomotives Built by Lima."

__, Vol. 106, No. 7, Feb. 12, 1944, "Central of Georgia Locomotives."

__, Misc. Issue pertaining to characteristics of various railroads, operations, motive power, etc.

Modeltech Magazine, August, 1994, "A Near Perfect Ten."

Railway Mechanical Engineer, May, 1942, "C&O 2-6-6-6 Locomotives."

__, March, 1944, "Central of Georgia 4-8-4 Type Locomotives."

__, August 1944, "C. & O. 2-8-4 Locomotives"

__, January, 1940, "2-8-8-4 Locomotives for S. P."

Railway Locomotive & Engineering, Vol. 38, No. 5, May 1925, "A 2-8-4 Locomotive for the Boston & Albany R. R."

__, Vol. 38, No. 6, May, 1925, "Fundamental Fuel Factors."

__, Vol. 38, No. 10, October, 1925, "Service Tests of the Lima 2-8-4 Locomotive."

Locomotive Quarterly, Vol. 1, No. 1, Fall 1987, "Central of Georgia Locomotives."

__, Vol. 10, No. 1, Fall 1986, "Engines of the Richmond, Fredericksburg & Potomac."

Chesapeake & Ohio Historical Newsletter & Magazine, Various issues.

Lima Loco Works "Photo Cards," showing photo of locomotive and backed with principal dimensions, misc. Issues from Collection of Kevin Kohls.

Trains, October, 1962, "The Engines That Saved a Railroad," by John A. Rehor.

Nickel Plate R

Built by the Lima

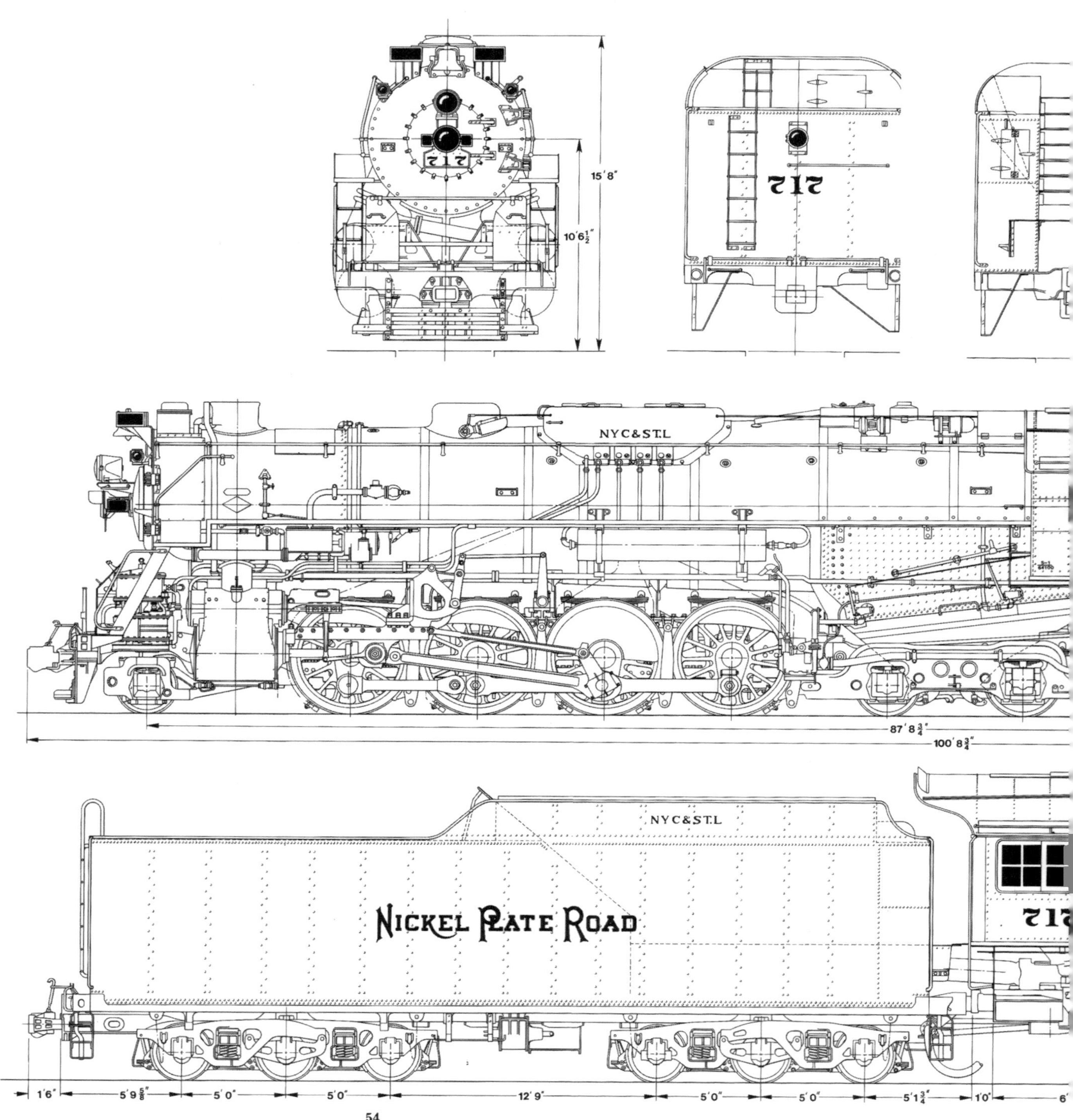